Negotiating with Faith

Islamic Strategies for Achieving Successful & Ethical Deals based on Sunnah Wisdom

SARAH GULFRAZ

Copyright © 2024 Sarah Gulfraz

Sarah Gulfraz has asserted her right to be identified as the author of this Work in accordance with the Copyright, Designs and Patents Act 1988.

All rights reserved.

No portion of this book may be reproduced in any form, stored in a retrieval system, stored in a database, or published/transmitted in any form or by any means, electronic, mechanical, photocopying, recording or otherwise, without prior written permission of the publisher.

Dedication

~ Bismillah ~

May Allah (swt) accept our efforts and grant us success in this life and the next. Ameen.

In dedication to my loving family and all their support.

Contents

1. Introduction to Negotiation in the Islamic Context — 1
2. Essential Principles of Islamic Negotiation — 14
3. Preparation and Planning for Successful Negotiations — 31
4. Effective Communication Skills in Negotiation — 44
5. Conflict Resolution and Mediation — 62
6. Negotiation Tactics and Strategies — 78
7. Ethics of Contractual Agreements — 93
8. Negotiating Halal Business Transactions — 105
9. Advancing Negotiation Skills through Faith and Practice — 116
10. Conclusion — 122

Find Out More — 124

Chapter 1
Introduction to Negotiation in the Islamic Context

Understanding the Importance of Negotiation in Islam

Conversations and talks aimed at reaching mutually beneficial deals or solutions within different areas of a business relationship or operation are called "business negotiations."

These talks can involve individuals, groups, or organisations and employ compromise and bargaining to get what these people want. Through smart talk, negotiation can settle a disagreement that works for all parties involved. Typically, this usually involves one or both sides giving up certain things.

In business, negotiation is the process of communicating, exchanging information, solving problems, and making decisions to reach an understanding or consensus that meets the needs and goals of all parties. In the context of Islamic teachings, negotiation carries additional layers of meaning and ethical considerations rooted in religious principles.

Islam sees negotiation as a decision-making process involving discussions amongst people to reach profitable agreements in their personal or professional lives. The word "negotiation" comes from the Latin *negotiare*, which means "to do business, trade, or deal".

Modern Latin languages have kept this original commercial connotation. For instance, *negozio* in Italian refers to a shop. Moreover, in the seventeenth and eighteenth centuries, "negotiate" denoted "to traffic in goods," underscoring its association with commerce. In brief, Islam encourages negotiation in business as a kind of conversation to achieve harmonious agreements and build connections that will benefit all parties involved.

In the light of Islamic teachings, negotiation in business plays a key role in deals among the parties as it promotes fair dealings, as Islam is a religion of peace and harmony.

> *In the Quran, Allah says, "Woe to those who give less [than due], who, when they take a measure from people, take in full. But if they give by measure or by weight to them, they cause loss." (Quran 83:1-3)*

In addition to this, when Allah (SWT) commanded Moses and Aaron to approach Pharaoh, he ordered them to speak gently, saying:

> *"Go, both of you, to Firaun (Pharaoh), verily he has transgressed (all bounds in disbelief and disobedience*

and behaved as an arrogant and as a tyrant) and speak to him mildly, perhaps he may accept admonition or fear Allah" (Quran 20:43-44)

Both the Quranic verse and the Hadith advocate honesty, transparency, and fairness, which are crucial for ethical negotiation and conduct in business. Furthermore, negotiating is a useful strategy for establishing, reaffirming, or facilitating friendly and cooperative relationships.

It's evident from these passages that Islam has taught Muslims communication and negotiation skills, providing some guidance on negotiation techniques. However, are these practices properly defined? Thus, the goal of this book is to examine this concept from an Islamic perspective. Let's explore!

The Concept of the Shariah-Compliant Negotiation Principles

A defining feature of the 21st century is the widespread adoption of the Islamic management system by an increasing number of Islamic businesses. Various groups have implemented this Islamic way of running companies, driven by the desire to follow Shariah rule.

However, these Islamic groups engage in talks and collaborations both externally with outsiders and internally among themselves to advance their interests and protect their domains. Because of this, understanding the Shariah rules they apply when dealing with different clients is very important.

As soon as people disagree, one of the first actions they take – something they do almost every day – is to negotiate. Negotiation is thought of as a set of serious, direct discussions between Muslims (or anyone else) to make friends, trade goods and services, figure out what's right and wrong, and settle conflicts calmly, all while adhering to Islamic values and rules.

Many scholars and points of view have examined the concept of negotiation from various perspectives. When it comes to Shariah, it's important to consider Islam's perspectives and goals dating back to the time of the Prophet Muhammad (PBUH).

The Quran contains ideas that can be used to create a fair and peaceful society, and through his Sunnah, or way of life, the Prophet Muhammad (PBUH) demonstrated these principles. These ideas shape every part of a Muslim's life.

Talks that follow Shariah are based on Islamic rule. Islamic groups and mosques need to recognise the importance of this rule if they want to follow it and achieve the best results now and in the future. Typically, those who agree on Shariah also agree on the Quran and Sunnah. According to this idea, discussions and agreements can't involve anything against Shariah law. This means that if you're Muslim, you can't talk about or engage in anything illegal or against Shariah.

What does Shariah actually mean? Well, Shariah is an Arabic word that means "a way to get water" or "a path to follow." Muslims understand the importance of being fair, decent, and good. In essence, Shariah law is the foundation that guides many aspects of a Muslim's life.

Shariah is a set of rules based on the Quran, the most important book in Islam, and the Sunnah, which are the teachings of the Prophet Muhammad (PBUH).

Discussions can't happen if Shariah opposes the matter. This means that the rules and the discussions should be aligned.

The Quran and Sunnah tell us how to deal in an Islamic way. Shariah says that something must follow Islamic law and ideas. It has to be based on the Quran and Sunnah and follow Islamic law.

The Concept of Negotiation in Islam

Fundamentally, Muslims believe that Islam is a comprehensive way of life that offers guidance in both religious matters and day-to-day activities like bargaining. Islam significantly impacts how negotiations are used in Islamic organisations and society.

In general, humans need to negotiate regularly to obtain their desired outcomes peacefully. Their answers highlighted three key ideas from the Islamic negotiation platforms, discussed below.

Reconciliation (Sulh)

Muslims employed the concept of reconciliation, or "*Sulh*," as a starting point for discussions. Based on my humble interpretation of the Quran and Sunnah, the term *Sulh* is typically used in the Quran to refer to negotiation. Islam urges all Muslims to engage in *Sulh* whenever there's a conflict to bring about mutual understanding, affection, harmony, and peace.

Sulh literally refers to compromise, amicable resolution, arbitration, conciliation, negotiation, and reconciliation. It often refers to the removal of conflicts and the introduction of goodness, justice, love, harmony, and peace.

The concept in the Quran, Allah (SWT) says in Surah Al-Nisa:

> *"There is no good in most of their secret talks save (in) him who orders Sadaqah (charity in Allah's Cause) or Maruf (Islamic Monotheism and all the good and righteous deeds which Allah has ordained) or concili-*

ation between mankind and he who does this, seeking the good Pleasure of Allah, We shall give him a great reward." (Quran, 4:114)

Moreover, in different places in the Quran, Allah talked about negotiation as:

"... and reconciliation is better. And human inner-selves are swayed by greed. But if you do well and keep away from evil, verily, Allah is Ever Well-Acquainted with what you do." (Quran, 4:128)

"They ask you (O Muhammad SAW) about the spoils of war. Say, 'The spoils are for Allah and the Messenger.' So fear Allah and adjust all matters of difference among you, and obey Allah and His Messenger (Muhammad SAW) if you are believers." (Quran, 8:1)

"So whosoever believes and does righteous good deeds, upon such shall come no fear, nor shall they grieve." (Surah Al-Annam)

It's affirmed and advised by the Quranic verses mentioned above to utilise the idea of *Sulh* as a foundation for resolving conflicts of any kind. They cited several Hadiths to support their claims, including one from Kathir bin Amr bin Awf Al-Muzani, who related from his father and grandfather that the Prophet Muhammad (PBUH) said:

> "*Reconciliation is allowed among the Muslims, except for reconciliation that makes the lawful unlawful or the unlawful lawful. And the Muslims will be held to their conditions, except the conditions that make the lawful unlawful or the unlawful lawful.*" (Tirmidhi)

In another Hadith, the Prophet Muhammad (PBUH) said that those who create *Sulh* among people will receive blessings. According to Abu Huraira, the Apostle of Allah:

> "*There is a Sadaqah to be given for every joint of the human body, and for every day on which the sun rises, there is a reward of a Sadaqah (i.e., charitable gift) for the one who establishes justice among people.*" (Sahih Al-Bukhari)

Sulh has been used by the Prophet Muhammad (PBUH) in numerous circumstances. For instance, according to the Prophet (PBUH), the Quba tribe once engaged in combat until they were covered in stone. Upon learning of it, Allah's Apostle said:

> "*Let us go to bring about reconciliation between them,*" Narrated Sahl bin Sad. (Sahih Al-Bukhari)

All of the Prophets (PBUH) preferred to conduct negotiations. These discussions have taken place throughout the history of the Prophethood and have been recorded at various points in the Quranic narratives and history.

Discussion and Consultation (Shurah)

The other is called *"Shurah"* (conversation, consultation), and it serves as a forum for talks. The Arabic term *Shurah* signifies "consultation" or "deliberation," referring to the process of reaching a decision through discussion and deliberation. Understanding the concept of *Shurah* is crucial for grasping the nature of negotiations, as it forms the foundational basis for these discussions.

> *"And those who answer the Call of their Lord, i.e., to believe that He is the only One Lord (Allah) and to worship none but Him Alone] and perform As-Salat (Iqamat-as-Salat) and who (conduct) their affairs by mutual consultation and who spend of what we have bestowed on them." (Quran, 42:38)*

The verse demonstrated how the principle of consultation is founded on issues concerning Muslim affairs not explicitly mentioned in Shariah law. As such, the basis of *Shurah* is extremely basic. If this culture of consultation is not present at every level, we should give up on negotiations.

Communication

Communication is the final sub-theme used in the discussions, following *Sulh* and *Shurah*. Islamic bargaining can be seen as a means by which both parties may communicate to arrive at a mutually beneficial objective for all parties involved.

As a consequence, Islam places great importance on various modes of communication and contains many fundamental laws that are closely associated with discussion, such as bargaining. It's essential for the *"ulama"* (scholars) or leaders of the Ummah to engage in discourse and debate with one another for Islam to be a religion that is founded on dialogue.

The Holy Quran and the Sunnah include several instances of bargaining based on this pattern. This is because of the circumstances described above. Each chapter has a conversation that pertains to them, such as the conversation between Ibrahim (PBUH) and Namrud or Musa (PBUH) and Firaun.

The above remarks show that the Sunnah and the Holy Quran have complete authority over every aspect of life and place great significance on every interaction we use daily. According to Islam, communication is vitally necessary for parties involved in a transaction.

Role of Prophetic Traditions in Developing Negotiation Skills

Muslims regard the Prophet Muhammad (PBUH) as the final Prophet. Allah (SWT) gave him the last instruction, the Holy Quran, for all humanity. It is supposed to remain relevant and applicable until the end of time. Muslims also believe that he (PBUH) was a flawless individual, sent by Allah (SWT) as a gift to humanity.

Muslims uphold that the Prophet's life established a notable example, inspiring people to emulate his negotiation techniques. He is revered as the ultimate role model, as mentioned in the Quran when Allah (SW) states:

> *"Indeed, in the Messenger of Allah (Muhammad SAW) you have a good example to follow for him who hopes in (the Meeting with) Allah and the Last Day and remembers Allah much." (Quran, 33:21)*

Because the Prophet Muhammad (PBUH) engaged in numerous negotiations with people from the outset of the Da'wah or when he first invited them to Islam, we can find a wealth of guidance and principles from Prophetic traditions—particularly from the Islamic tradition—that can be applied to the development of negotiation skills in the Sunnah. Let's explore this in detail!

Learning from the Negotiation Tactics of the Prophet

Here are some ways in which these traditions can contribute to effective negotiation:

1. Emphasis on Ethics and Integrity

Prophetic traditions value morality, ethics, and honesty. Integrity is, in short, a crucial component of fruitful negotiations. It supports ethical norms, cultivates positive relationships, aids in problem-solving, helps establish trust, and may even help avert legal problems.

Integrity is the first priority in negotiations, and this helps parties establish a favourable atmosphere for coming to advantageous agreements. The Prophet Muhammad (PBUH), for instance, said:

> *"The truthful and trustworthy merchant is with the Prophets, the truthful, and the martyrs." (Tirmidhi)*

This verse emphasises how crucial honesty is in all of your interactions.

2. Patience and Perseverance

Negotiations are usually tough and take a long time. Patience is one of the most important traits of a good mediator. Time is the same as patience; longer talks might produce better results. Patience is the best way to negotiate because it gives you time. It takes time to fully understand the deal and its risks. Prophetic cultures encourage people to be patient and persistent, which are essential traits for successful talks.

> *The Prophet Muhammad (PBUH) said: "May Allah show mercy to a man who adopts a kind manner when he sells, buys, and demands for the repayment of loans."*
> *(Sahih Al-Bukhari)*

This hadith emphasises the value of patience, especially in negotiations and dealings with others.

3. Effective Communication

Effective communication is the key to successful negotiations, helping individuals find common ground, express their own needs, and see things from the perspectives of others. Communicating politely, clearly, and concisely fosters collaborations and cultivates a nice atmosphere. The Prophet Muhammad (PBUH) emphasised the importance of knowing and listening to other people's points of view when bargaining. He was renowned for clearly explaining his thoughts and speaking with style.

> For instance, the Prophet said, "The best of you is the one who is best in his dealings with others." (Sahih Al-Bukhari)

4. Seeking Mutual Benefit

Prophetic traditions encourage solutions that are good for all parties rather than some one-sided advantage. There are numerous hadiths with practical applications of the general principle of justice. Prophet Muhammad (PBUH) was always honest in his dealings with others, even before his Prophethood.

> As he said: "Trying to earn a lawful livelihood is an obligatory duty in addition to the duties which are obligatory." (Mishkatul Miasabi)

5. Flexibility and Compromise

The Prophet Muhammad (PBUH) used these qualities in his dealings in general, for example, in the Treaty of Hudaybiyyah, where he showed tremendous flexibility in negotiating peace.

6. Building Relationships

Building strong, positive relationships is a key element in successful negotiations. Prophetic traditions emphasise the importance of maintaining good relationships and treating others with kindness and respect.

> The Prophet Muhammad (PBUH) said, "The best of you are those who are best to their families" (Tirmidhi)

Hence, the prophetic traditions present a complete set of skills for developing effective negotiation. The above-mentioned timeless values are valued in personal and professional negotiations and contribute to building a more just and pleasant-sounding society.

In business and everything we do, it's best to always act with fairness. This is exactly what the Sunnah teaches. When we treat each other fairly, Allah blesses our affairs with *"Barakah"* (blessing). The principle of fairness is an essential component of economic transactions because it guarantees that all parties involved are treated justly and fairly. When it comes to a company's reputation, fairness is crucial as it builds trust, prevents misunderstandings and disagreements, and helps uphold that reputation.

Chapter 2
Essential Principles of Islamic Negotiation

Adhering to Islamic Ethics in Negotiation

Negotiation success is usually a prerequisite for business success. Ethics play a crucial role in negotiations, providing a framework for acting morally, honestly, and fairly. This ethical framework ensures that all parties are treated with respect and integrity at all times.

Upholding Basic Principles in Negotiation Processes

Applying Islamic ethics in negotiation links Islam's teachings with how negotiation is conducted. Based on the Quranic and Hadithic foundations, these principles promote fair dealings. Below are a couple of core concepts to guide you in navigating ethical considerations in common negotiation settings grounded in Islam:

Adaptability to negotiate

Recognising the freedom and rights of the opposing party to negotiate is the cornerstone of the Islamic approach to negotiation. Every discussed problem might be viewed differently from the correct and wrong angles since various people belong to different schools of thought. If negotiations were coerced, they would never succeed. Therefore, willingness to compromise is one of the most important factors for successful negotiation and transactions.

From the Islamic perspective, coercing another party into negotiations is unacceptable. Each individual or organisation is accountable for their own behaviour and actions during negotiations.

Sincerity (Ikhlas)

Sincerity *"Ikhlas"* is another crucial sub-principle for the Quran and Sunnah principles. Being sincere is acting with the sole purpose of pleasing Allah (SWT) without looking to others for praise. This includes both talks and deeds. Being honest means eschewing any bad intentions that corrupt people's words and deeds. Since Allah is the only one who knows people's intentions and sincerity, sincerity plays a crucial role in evaluating one's actions in Islam.

Putting *Ikhlas* and good intentions into practice is crucial. Most of those who negotiate typically have predetermined goals, and the results are not favourable. However, with sincerity, negotiations will ultimately succeed, earning Allah's (SWT) approval. Ultimately, the goal is to succeed for Allah's sake (SWT). We must comprehend the negotiating mandate precisely since any ambiguity would render the negotiation process futile.

Furthermore, being sincere in a Shariah-compliant negotiation implies entering discussions with an open mind and honesty. Success in bargaining comes from staying true to yourself and having faith in Allah (SWT). To ensure that the negotiation's end is successful, the Shariah-complaint negotiation is, in fact, primarily predicated on the principles of sincerity and good intention.

Righteousness

From an Islamic perspective, fairness is yet another fundamental tenet of negotiating. In Islam, justice might signify different things, but it always refers to putting things in their rightful positions. In economic dealings, Islam demands complete justice and fairness. It teaches that a deal isn't honourable if one compromises one's religion and forfeits blessings from Allah for financial gain. A Muslim would never accept such a compromise.

Therefore, you must treat people fairly to seek justice for yourself. In Islam, fair negotiation is imperative since Allah (SWT) has commanded us to do so, saying as follows:

> *"Verily, Allah enjoins Al-Adl (i.e. justice and worshipping none but Allah Alone-Islamic Monotheism) and Al-Ihsan [i.e. to be patient in performing your duties to Allah, totally for Allah's sake and in accordance with the Sunnah (legal ways) of the Prophet (PBUH) in a perfect manner] and giving (help) to kith and kin (i.e. all that Allah has ordered you to give them e.g., wealth, visiting, looking after them, or any other kind of help, etc.): and forbids Al- Fahsha' (i.e. all evil deeds, e.g. illegal sexual acts, disobedience of parents, polytheism, to tell lies, to give false witness, to kill a life without right, etc.) and Al-Munkar (i.e. all that is prohibited by Islamic law: polytheism of every kind, disbelief and every kind of evil deeds, etc.) and Al-Baghy (i.e. all*

kinds of oppression, He admonishes you, that you may take heed." (Quran, 16:90)

"O you who believe, Stand out firmly for Allah and be just witnesses and let not the enmity and hatred of others make you avoid justice. Be just: that is nearer to piety and fear Allah. Verily, Allah is Well-acquainted with what you do." (Quran, 5:8)

It's evident from the aforementioned verses in the Quran that Allah (SWT) views justice as the highest value and the fundamental goal of Islam. Thus, justice is a fundamental tenet of bargaining, and Islam places a strong emphasis on it. As a result, we must make every effort to practice justice, which entails avoiding extremes, being reasonable, and arranging matters in the proper order. Allah (SWT) commands us to always act justly in Surah Al-Hujurat of the Holy Quran.

"And if two parties or groups among the believers fall to fighting, then make peace between them both, but if one of them rebels against the other, then fight you (all) against the one that which rebels till it complies with the Command of Allah, then if it complies, then make reconciliation between them justly and be equitable. Verily! Allah loves those who are equitable." (Quran, 49:9)

The idea of justice in Shariah-complaint negotiation is defined as "to give the equal right to all, including your enemies," and "do not misuse someone else's right or interest."

This is due to Islam's prohibition of injustice and oppression, as made abundantly clear in the genuine Hadith of the Prophet Muhammad (PBUH), as reported by Abu Dharr: Allah's Messenger (PBUH) delivered that Allah, the Exalted and Glorious, said:

> "My servants, I have made oppression unlawful for Me and unlawful for you, so do not commit oppression against one another" (Sahih Muslim)

Equity

Fairness is a crucial tenet in Shariah-compliant negotiations. It's believed that negotiations are destined to fail without the fair treatment of all parties involved. Fairness entails respecting the rights of all parties during negotiations. This principle must be upheld in every interaction. The negotiating parties should always be treated fairly in Shariah-compliant talks since, according to Islam, all persons are equal and deserve justice.

While justice is about giving everyone the same rights, fairness involves considering how you would want to be treated if roles were reversed. In essence, justice is about impartiality and the absence of prejudice against certain groups or persons. Giving each individual their rightful due is justice in a broader sense.

Islam strongly emphasises the idea of fairness. In his intertribal negotiations, the Prophet Muhammad (PBUH) always made sure to treat both equally. This philosophy ensured that any deals could be closed without tyranny or unfairness.

Win-win: It goes without saying that the purpose of negotiation is to prevail or reach what is considered a fair outcome. In particular, from an Islamic standpoint, the talks have objectives, but in the end, one or more of the negotiating sides emerge victorious.

"It means a platform to put both sides on without a major sacrifice, but at the end of the day, we reach a win-win situation." The discussion around Shariah complaints is based on justice and equity in all transactions. This is so because Islam forbids its adherents from violating the rights of others, not even those of individuals of different faiths. If they act in this way, it is against Islamic law and a sin.

The purpose of Islam is to enable its obedient adherents to have lives that are abundant in every meaning of the word. This is seen, for instance, in a verse where Allah tells His Prophet (PBUH) how to handle and negotiate with humanity if necessary. According to Ibn Kathir's interpretation, Allah says,

> "And argue with them in a way that is best" (Surat An-Nahl). He tells his Prophet ((PBUH)) if any of them (mankind) had to talk and debate, do it gently, and with a good speech translation of the meaning in this dimension is that negotiation is ordered by Allah (SWT). (Quran, 16:125)

Studies of the Prophet Muhammad (PBUH) often highlight his exemplary negotiation skills. His life is full of examples where his negotiating abilities were essential in determining how things turned out.

The Prophet (PBUH) was the most pleasant person to deal with and had the kindest attitude of everyone when he bought, sold, or demanded payment. May Allah's peace and blessings be upon him. He wasn't interested in earthly things, nor was buying or selling his main concern.

But he would stroll about the marketplaces, buying and selling, teaching others the manners of trade and the attributes a merchant should have—honesty, self-control, dependability, kindness, and love for people—both by word and deed. As a Sunnah practice in Islam, negotiation embodies the values of justice, diplomacy, and respect for one another, as demonstrated by the Prophet Muhammad (PBUH).

Authenticity

The idea behind this principle is the commitment to honesty in words and deeds, a virtue in line with nature. This idea is crucial to carrying out a successful negotiation and for any human interaction. The remaining three tenets of credibility are truth, respect, and honesty.

1. **Honesty (Amanah)**

Amanah is the Arabic term for honesty, literally meaning "trust, validity, reliability, devotion, fidelity, and integrity." Sincerity, the first sub-principle of believability, is highly valued in Islam and forms one of the pillars of the faith. Islam, therefore, regards this idea as the believers' moral fortitude.

> *"Those who are faithfully true to their Amanah (all the duties which Allah has ordained, honesty, moral responsibility and trusts etc.) and to their covenants..."* (Quran, 23:8)

> *"And those who keep their trusts and covenants"*
> *(Quran, 70:32)*

If being honest is one of the tenets of Islam, then it's also a fundamental component of equitable negotiation. This is so because the Amanah serves as the link between all parties. When negotiating, you must be truthful in explaining and accepting opposing viewpoints. In another way, honesty in this context refers to being truthful in every situation.

Furthermore, from an Islamic perspective, honesty also refers to keeping one's word, whether verbally or in writing, in both text and spirit. Muslims are commanded by Islam to always be honest and to uphold their commitments and contracts. That this is made abundantly evident in the subsequent verses:

> *"O you who believe...Fulfill (your) obligations" (Quran, 5:1)*

2. Respect

Respect is the second sub-principle of believability. In negotiations, there are two common interpretations of it. One concentrates on a person's inner emotions, while the other on his outward deeds.

Take and give are always important considerations in negotiations, anchored in Shariah-complaint ethics where mutual understanding and non-offensive communication prevail.

Everything has a purpose for which it was created, so everything deserves respect. You must respect the other party and honour their rights, regardless of who they are or where they are from. This is so because one of the cornerstones of Islamic principles is respect.

Respecting others' rights is a trust that can't be broken. Violating these rights can lead to disputes within humanity, which is extremely problematic for all parties involved.

Consequently, it's critical to concentrate on the importance of this auxiliary principle in Shariah-complaint discussions.

3. Truth

The final sub-principle relates to trustworthiness. In negotiations, each party is interested in the truth since accurate information is necessary for making informed decisions.

In Islam, truth goes beyond just speaking with integrity; it's the alignment of the outward with the inward, the action and the intention, the word and the conviction, and the practice and the teaching.

For negotiations to truly succeed, all parties must be true to each other to negotiate and find common ground.

Islam commands its adherents to identify with the truth throughout history. Allah (SW) states:

> *"O you who believe... Be afraid of Allah and be with those who are true (in words and deeds)" (Quran, 9:119)*

> *From the Sunnah, Abdullah bin Masud reported that Allah's Messenger (PBUH) said: "Telling of truth is a virtue and virtue leads to Paradise and the servant who endeavours, to tell the truth, is recorded as truthful and lie is obscenity and obscenity leads to Hell-Fire and the servant who endeavours to tell a lie is recorded as a liar" (Sahih Muslim)*

In this genuine Hadith, the Prophet Muhammad (PBUH) affirms that Muslims must always tell the truth. Virtue leads to Paradise, and practising honesty brings rewards, with Muslims who adhere to truthfulness being recognised as truthful by Allah. Conversely, unethical behaviours, such as lying, making unfulfilled promises, cheating, or deceiving others, are condemned as false and lead to negative consequences.

However, He (PBUH) forbade Muslims from lying because lying breeds obscenity, and obscenity breeds Hellfire. Furthermore, a person who consistently tells lies is considered a liar by Allah.

> *Allah's Messenger (PBUH) said: "Both parties in a business transaction... if they speak the truth and make everything clear they will be blessed in their transaction, but if they tell a lie and conceal anything the blessing on their transaction will be blotted out." (Sahih Muslim)*

Yes, if the truth is the key to all the doors of virtue that could lead to paradise in Islam, it's also essential to any negotiation's success.

Avoiding Deception and Manipulation in Business Deals

Avoiding deception and manipulation in business deals is crucial for maintaining integrity, trust, and long-term success. Islam greatly supports legal economic ventures because they directly and considerably raise people's living standards. In whatever they do, Muslims are commanded to conduct with devotion and fear of Allah, for in Islam, transactions driven by avarice, exploitation, or the desire to amass profit are forbidden.

Nonetheless, Islam detests deceit, fraud, and financial exploitation in commerce and other social interactions since it's a religion that governs, eases, and guides life in all of its aspects. Because the foundation of a good Islamic civilisation is honesty, justice, fairness, fraternity, and a fear of Allah, the Holy Prophet Muhammad (PBUH) stressed the need to have positive traits in our economic dealings and interpersonal relationships.

Definition of Deception (Al-Gaish)

By presenting information to support a false view that is known or really thought to be incorrect, one might purposefully lead someone else to hold or maintain a false belief. This is known as deceit. It's a deliberate act intended to deceive by profiting from the naivete or innocence of others.

There's no room for commercial deceit or cheating if the business is conducted strictly in line with the Islamic principles of commerce. This includes profiteering, which can range from the most subtle and cunning to the most obvious, all of which are often covered under the pretence of honesty.

While there are many ways to be dishonest or cheat, one prevalent practice is hiding product flaws or misleading consumers about a product's quality, components, weight, number, or other crucial details.

Cheating is strictly prohibited, as demonstrated by several passages and texts in the Quran and the Sunnah (the Hadith). This applies to both Muslims and non-Muslims. The Almighty Allah has forbidden lying, and those who commit it in the Holy Quran threaten them with dire repercussions.

The Holy Quran emphasises the value of justice in business, and several pertinent verses provide directives that forbid any dishonest or unfair dealings. The following verses clarify this further:

> "*Woe to those who give less [than due]; Who, when they take a measure from people, take in full; But if they give by measure or by weight to them, they cause loss; Do they not think that they will be resurrected; For a tremendous Day; The Day when mankind will stand before the Lord of the worlds?" (Quran, 83:1-6)*

Islam prohibits lying, cheating, and deceit in all of its forms, whether the parties involved are Muslims or not. The Holy Quran emphasises the importance of justice in business:

> "*And, O my people, gives full measure and weight justly and defrauds not men of their things, and act not corruptly in the land making mischief. What remains with Allah is better for you if you are believers" (Quran, 11:85-86)*

According to another passage in the Holy Quran, Prophet Shuaib (AS) was speaking to his people when he remarked,

> "*O my people! Serve Allah, you have no God other than Him, and do not give short measure and weight. Surely I see you in prosperity, and surely I fear for you the punishment of an all-encompassing day. And O my people! Give full measure and weight fairly, and defraud not men their things, and do not act corruptly in the land, making mischief." (Quran, 11:84-85)*

Nonetheless, Islam detests deceit, fraud, and financial exploitation in commerce and other social interactions since it's a religion that governs, eases, and guides life in all of its aspects. Because the foundation of a good Islamic civilisation is honesty, justice, fairness, fraternity, and a fear of Allah, the Holy Prophet Muhammad (PBUH) stressed the need to have positive traits in our economic dealings and interpersonal relationships.

Before turning to trade or business as a career, Muslims must obtain sufficient information and deep comprehension of the regulations governing business dealings in Islam. Using deceptive, exploitative, and corrupting techniques to influence people is morally unacceptable. The Prophet Muhammad (PBUH) chastised dishonest merchants and companies by saying:

> *"Whosoever deceives us is not one of us." (Sunan Ibn Majah)*

This serves as a severe warning against lying and cheating, as anyone who doesn't belong to the followers of Prophet Muhammad (PBUH) would perish in the afterlife.

Along with abstaining from defrauding one another, people have been advised to honour their duties to Allah and the Holy Prophets by abstaining from cheating and deceiving one another.

This is founded on the idea that Allah (SWT) endows man with infinite favours. He grants his requests, considers his well-being, and pays attention to his pleas.

Thus, it's the responsibility of man to obey and fulfil his duty toward Allah (SWT) by showing gratitude for His blessings and by adhering to His commands. Islam disapproves of any form of dishonest behaviour.

> *The Holy Prophet Muhammad (PBUH) said: "The buyers and sellers are free till they do not separate, and if they have acted with honesty and have explained the defects of commodities, then Allah will bless them with prosperity. And if both of them tried to deal dishonestly and tried to hide the defects then it is likely that they may get some profit, but the prosperity will vanish from their trade" (Sahih Muslim)*

Before turning to engage in trade or business as a career, Muslims must obtain sufficient information and a deep comprehension of the regulations governing business dealings in Islam.

Using deceptive, exploitative, and corrupting techniques to influence people is morally unacceptable. The Prophet Muhammad (PBUH) chastised dishonest merchants and companies by saying:

> *"Whosoever deceives us is not one of us." (Ibn Majah)*

This serves as a severe warning against lying and cheating, as anyone who doesn't belong to the followers of Prophet Muhammad (PBUH) will perish in the afterlife.

Based on the submission above, it's evident that most ethical notions and standards in business and interactions are rooted in Islamic doctrine.

The lesson here is that since Muslim culture is built on sincerity toward all Muslims, purity of sensation, love, and keeping pledges made to all members of society, lying and deception are abhorrent behaviours.

Building Trust and Rapport with Negotiation Partners

Establishing relationships is the primary goal of negotiation, not merely making agreements and concessions. Any effective negotiation has trust at its core. When it comes to negotiating costs, settling conflicts, or overcoming obstacles at work, trust is the glue that keeps everything together. Any negotiation's basis of trust starts with building a relationship between the parties.

Developing a rapport between negotiators entails making them feel understood and connected. Finding common ground, demonstrating empathy, and engaging in active listening help achieve this.

Negotiators show that they appreciate the relationship and are dedicated to reaching a mutually beneficial agreement by attentively listening to their wants and desires. Expressing a sincere interest in the other person's viewpoint and worries is a good method of building rapport. Furthermore, empathetic behaviour toward the difficulties faced by the other side might aid in mending rifts and developing rapport.

Negotiators who view one another as partners rather than opponents are more inclined to approach negotiations with collaboration and transparency. Discovering points of agreement is yet another crucial component of building rapport. Establishing common objectives, principles, or life experiences can foster cohesion and cooperation, paving the way for developing trust.

To establish confidence during negotiations, one must be trustworthy and consistent. When both parties can count on one another to act consistently and keep their word, they are more inclined to trust one another. Reliability builds trust in the sincerity and intentions of the other person.

Another essential component of developing trust in negotiations is reliability. Reliability and keeping one's word improve one's perceived trustworthiness. This can be proven by answering messages right away, keeping one's word, and fulfilling commitments. By persistently exhibiting dependability, negotiators can foster trust by instilling confidence in their capacity to fulfil their commitments.

> *"The Prophet (PBUH) said: 'the best of people are those who are most beneficial to people.'" (Al-Mujam Al-Awsat)*

Consistency in negotiations requires a consistent demeanour and matching words with deeds. Promises made during negotiations should be kept, deadlines met, and agreements carried out. Maintaining consistency in one's actions establishes credibility and gives the opposing side confidence in the negotiation procedure.

A key component of a fruitful negotiation is trust. By building rapport and exhibiting consistency and dependability, negotiators can foster an atmosphere of trust and facilitate the creation of mutually beneficial agreements. Parties can cultivate trust, improve cooperation, and attain the best results in their negotiating strategy.

> *"Verily... Allah commands that you should render back the trusts to those, to whom they are due; and that when you judge between men, you judge with justice. Verily, how excellent is the teaching which He (Allah) gives you!*

Truly, Allah is Ever All Hearers, All Seers" (Quran, 4:58)

Chapter 3
Preparation and Planning for Successful Negotiations

Importance of Preparation in Islamic Negotiation

There are many different reasons why people negotiate, including to settle a conflict, obtain a better bargain, or develop novel solutions that neither side could have come up with on their own. Beyond what negotiators ought to do before a negotiation, planning and preparation are essential. Negotiators should also be ready to handle unforeseen circumstances and obstacles because negotiation is a continuous communication process where new information, worries, emotions, and goals may surface.

Before starting any conversations, it's important to extensively research the parties involved, the market's state, and the transaction's particulars. Gaining an understanding of each party's objectives and demands can help you create suggestions that respect Islamic law while taking into account everyone's interests. Let's have a look in detail!

Conducting Research and Gathering Relevant Information Before Negotiations

The Holy Quran explicitly references research, which helps us understand the wisdom and truth of things and compels us to look into any topic. Islam's teachings state that conducting research is a means of obtaining information; in fact, one of a Muslim's obligations is to pursue knowledge. Numerous verses in the Quran and Hadith encourage Muslims to constantly broaden their knowledge and conduct research to better comprehend their personal and professional life.

In the Quran, Allah says:

> "O you who have believed, when you contract a debt for a specified term, write it down. And let a scribe write between you in justice. Let no scribe refuse to write as Allah has taught him. So let him write and let the one who has the obligation dictate. And let him fear Allah, his Lord, and not leave anything out of it. ... And bring to witness two witnesses from among your men and if there are not two men [available], then a man and two women from those whom you accept as witnesses - so that if one of the women errs, then the other can remind her. ... And do not be [too] weary to write it, whether it is small or large, for its [specified] term. That is more just in the sight of Allah and stronger as evidence and more likely to prevent doubt between you." (Quran, 2:282)

This verse emphasises the importance of recording and documenting transactions carefully, which implies a thorough understanding and preparation before engaging in business deals.

Moreover, the Hadith below highlights the need to fully understand a transaction or business enterprise, which calls for extensive research and due diligence before commencing any business dealings.

> *The Prophet Muhammad (PBUH) said: "It is obligatory upon a Muslim that he should not sell a thing unless he knows its full details." (Ibn Majah)*

Comparably, by realising the importance of studying, carrying out in-depth research, and applying the knowledge you have gained, you can improve your negotiating abilities and notably succeed in obtaining better agreements for your company. For the following reasons, research is extremely important in business negotiations:

Research provides valuable knowledge that can be used as leverage in talks. Parties can obtain a competitive edge by keeping abreast of market conditions, competition offerings, and industry trends. With this information, you may establish your company as a valuable partner, back up your assertions, and present strong cases for the requests you have made during negotiations.

Conducting thorough research about the company or negotiation partner can reveal their priorities, values, and objectives. Understanding their background allows you to adjust your negotiating strategy, communicate with them in their own language, and offer solutions that serve their needs.

Research also identifies areas where the company's objectives align with your aspirations. This realisation aids in concentrating on parts of the negotiation that will benefit parties, encouraging teamwork and raising the possibility of a successful resolution. By tailoring your suggestions to their unique needs and considering their opportunities, difficulties, and pain areas, you may increase the likelihood that they will accept your offers.

Furthermore, research equips you with the necessary information to make wise judgments when negotiating. Knowing the company's goals, difficulties, and priorities allows you to provide solutions that satisfy their demands when aligning with your objectives. Making well-informed decisions enhances your chances of identifying points of agreement and achieving win-win situations.

Getting to know the people you'll be negotiating with can help you find points of agreement, hobbies, or personal relationships. Establishing a good relationship and mutual trust is the first step towards collaborative work, clear communication, and efficient problem-solving. Strong connections can result in enduring collaborations, recurring business, and a network of supporters for your business.

Research is an essential element of fruitful business negotiations. Armed with insightful knowledge, you can confidently engage in negotiations, make wise choices, and negotiate better terms that benefit all sides. Your ability to negotiate and your company's success will benefit from the time and effort you put into your company's overall success. You may create deeper relationships, seize new chances, and accomplish amazing outcomes in your negotiation activities by utilising the power of research. Recall that information is power, which may hold the key to success in negotiations.

Setting Clear Goals and Objectives Aligned with Islamic Values

Integrating Islamic ethical concepts into the foundation of your business operations entails setting specific goals and objectives that align with the teachings of the Quran and the Sunnah in commercial relations. For a negotiation to be effective, you must set realistic goals.

In Islamic business activities, success is not the only goal, nor is exploiting others or engaging in ruthless rivalry. Rather, you must have a solid ethical foundation. As a Muslim, you understand that morality and ethics are at the heart of every business deal.

All Muslim business endeavours should be based on these principles to first establish a connection with Allah (SWT) and then pursue worldly gain through legal and lawful means as directed by Allah (SWT).

Your ultimate goal is to win Allah's favour and respect in the Hereafter. By establishing goals early in the negotiation process, you can determine your negotiation's plan of action, tactics, and reservation point—all of which can help avert less favourable terms.

Goal setting: An Islamic perspective

Negotiations risk becoming aimless without targets and goals, resulting in wasted opportunities, inadequate agreements, and diminished value. Setting goals in line with Islamic values and principles is the first stage in your goal-setting from an Islamic perspective. As a Muslim, you should establish objectives that support good deeds and behaviours consistent with the lessons found in the Quran and Hadith.

It's crucial to remember that in Islamic goal-setting, you shouldn't restrict yourself to egotistical or materialistic objectives. Islam encourages Muslims to develop goals that will help them in all facets of life, whether personal or professional. As a Muslim, you ought to make an effort to connect your objectives with the welfare of humanity as a whole.

> *The Prophet Muhammad (PBUH) said, "Verily, deeds are only with intentions, and every person will have only what they intended" (Sahih Al-Bukhari)*

It would be best if you also made a concerted effort to create SMART goals—specific, measurable, achievable, relevant, and time-bound. This methodology guarantees that your objectives are attainable, feasible, and amenable to monitoring and assessment. Setting SMART goals helps you stay motivated and focused and, more importantly, allows you to evaluate progress and adjust your strategy as needed. When you have clear goals, negotiations gain a distinct focus. Establishing goals and objectives makes it easier to set boundaries and expectations and ensures that everyone knows what is and isn't possible. It also helps manage expectations and ambitions and internally coordinate with others. This guarantees that all parties involved stay on course and avoid any misunderstandings that may arise throughout the negotiation process.

Because they are dynamic, negotiations may run into unforeseen problems. Therefore, it's critical to be ready to modify your goals as needed. Being flexible allows you to find win-win solutions and adjust to evolving situations. As you gather new information during negotiations, be willing to make flexible adjustments to your target sets and objectives.

In summary, Islamic goal-setting is a crucial component of negotiation. As a Muslim, you should establish objectives that support good deeds and behaviours consistent with Islamic teachings and are advantageous to all parties involved in business dealings. Your objectives should be defined with the purpose of gaining Allah's pleasure and bettering yourself. They should also be time-bound, relevant, quantifiable, attainable, and explicit.

In terms of setting and attaining goals, Prophet Muhammad (PBUH) is an excellent example for Muslims to follow. His life exemplifies the worth of setting goals consistent with one's religion and morals, the strength of tenacity, and the necessity of asking Allah for guidance to achieve those goals.

Applying Prophetic Strategies for Negotiation Preparation

Applying Prophetic strategies to negotiation preparation can offer a unique and effective approach. Here are some key strategies, each accompanied by relevant examples:

Self-Preparation and Clarity of Purpose

Prophets often spent time contemplating and preparing before their missions. For example, before the Hijra to Medina, Prophet Muhammad (PBUH) carefully planned and prepared for the migration, understanding the implications and challenges ahead.

Patience and Persistence

Prophets often faced challenges with patience and perseverance. In negotiations, this means staying calm and committed. For example, Prophet Ayyub (Job) was known for his patience during times of great trials.

Moral and Ethical Integrity

Prophets upheld strong moral and ethical standards. In negotiations, this meant maintaining honesty and fairness. For example, Prophet Yusuf was known for his integrity and fairness, Prophet Yusuf managed Egypt's resources judiciously during a famine.

Effective Communication

Prophets communicated their messages clearly and effectively. In negotiations, this means active listening and clear articulation. For example, Prophet Musa (AS) communicated effectively with the Pharaoh despite the challenges.

Prophet Sulaiman (AS): Prophets often demonstrated deep empathy and understanding. In negotiations, this involves understanding and addressing the other party's needs and emotions. For example, Prophet Muhammad (PBUH) is known for his compassion and understanding of people's needs.

Divine Guidance and Wisdom

Prophets sought divine guidance in their decisions. For religious individuals, incorporating this can offer additional insight and confidence. For example, Prophet Sulaiman (AS) is renowned for seeking divine wisdom.

Integrating these Prophetic strategies into your negotiation preparation can enhance your effectiveness, build stronger relationships, and achieve beneficial and just outcomes.

Seeking Guidance Through Prayer (Istikhara) and Consultation (Shura)

Translating from Arabic, *Istikhara* means "seeking guidance from Allah." Prophet Muhammad (PBUH) advised Muslims to recite the Istikhara supplication before embarking on any significant matter due to its importance.

Any action, regardless of size, has the potential to confuse a Muslim. The outcomes of their decisions ultimately rest with them. Hence, Dua-Istikhara was introduced – to seek clarity and make wise decisions by placing their trust in Allah.

Feelings of uncertainty as well as doubt are common during business negotiations. Muslims can gain a clear understanding of their way of action with the aid of Istikhara. The assurance that Allah will light the way also eases some anxiety and helps clear any confusion.

Performing Istikhara leads to better decision-making. It helps Muslims recognise Allah's signs and align their objectives with Islamic principles by beginning to rely entirely on Allah for all business matters. This contributes to the development of decision-making confidence in all business-related domains.

Istikhara is an expression of one's love for Allah, signifying submission to His will and instruction regardless of the choice made. It acknowledges that *Rizq* solely originates from Him and reinforces reliance on His wisdom, thereby nurturing a deeper connection with Allah. This connection can positively impact all areas of our lives, particularly business.

To conduct Istikhara before engaging in any significant business negotiations, follow this broad outline:

The two optional components (rakats) of the Istikhara prayer are offered with the goal of asking Allah for guidance at times other than those when prayer is forbidden. Istikhara is not limited to a set time; rather, it can be performed whenever one is troubled by something and seeks Allah's guidance on it.

During Istikhara, after reciting Surah Al-Fatiha in each rakat, individuals can recite any section of the Quran they wish. However, reciting "Surah Al-Kafirun" in the first unit and "Surah Al-Ikhlas" in the second is advised.

These choices represent genuine desire, sincere delegation, and acceptance of one's reliance on Allah. According to some scholars, certain verses should be added after Al-Fatiha in each unit. One may repeat the following in the first unit:

> "Your Lord creates whatever He wills, and He chooses. The choice is not theirs. Glory be to Allah, and exalted be He above the associations they make. And your Lord knows what their hearts conceal and what they reveal." (Quran 28:68-69)

In the second unit, the verse:

> "It is not for a believing man or a believing woman, when Allah and His Messenger have decided a matter, that they should [thereafter] have any choice about their affair. And whoever disobeys Allah and His Messenger has certainly strayed into clear error." (Quran 33:36)

The supplication:

> "O Allah, I seek Your guidance through Your knowledge, and I seek Your assistance through Your power, and I ask you from your immense bounty. Indeed, you have power, and I do not have power, and you know, and I do not know, and You are the Knower of the unseen.

> O Allah, if You know that this matter (mention your matter here) is good for me in terms of my religion, my livelihood, and the outcome of my affairs, then decree it

for me, facilitate it for me, and bless me in it. And if You know that this matter (mention your matter here) is bad for me in terms of my religion, my livelihood, and the outcome of my affairs, then turn it away from me, and turn me away from it, and decree for me what is good wherever it may be, and make me pleased with it."
(Sahih Al-Bukhari)

The petition should be given once the prayer is concluded, beginning with acclaim and exaltation. According to the Prophet Muhammad (PBUH):

"When one of you is considering a matter, let them pray two units of voluntary prayer (nafl) other than the obligatory prayers, then say: 'O Allah, I seek Your guidance through Your knowledge...' until the end." (Sahih Al-Bukhari)

It's customary to raise one's hands in suppliant supplication following the two units of prayer. However, one can also make this supplication during Sujood or right before completing prayer after Tashahud.

After completing the prayer, it's time to express one's specific request.

The Messenger of Allah states: "When one of you supplicates, let them begin by praising their Lord and adoring him, then sending blessings upon the Prophet

*(PBUH), then supplicating for whatever they wish."
(Tirmidhi)*

Utilising Wisdom (Hikmah) and Foresight in Negotiation Strategy

In Islamic negotiation methods, "*hikmah*" (wisdom) and foresight are essential components. Applying these deeply ingrained Islamic beliefs can guarantee just and productive talks.

Hikmah, or wisdom, is the ability to fully comprehend a situation or topic and make appropriate decisions based on a comprehension of cause-and-effect phenomena.

In his interactions, the Prophet Muhammad (PBUH) set an example of hikmah by acting with tolerance, compassion, and justice.

The definition of wisdom includes:

- The capacity for sound judgment and decision-making

- Making the most of the information at hand

- Anticipating outcomes and taking action to optimise positive outcomes

- Deciding what is best and acting accordingly in each particular circumstance

The Quran promotes applying wisdom:

> *"Invite to the way of your Lord with wisdom and good instruction, and argue with them in a way that is best."*
> *(Quran 16:125)*

Wisdom is a valuable asset that plays a significant role in negotiation. It's a deeply thoughtful approach to navigating life's intricate and ever-changing aspects. Integrating wisdom and foresight into negotiation strategies reflects a commitment to ethical, beneficial, and sustainable agreements.

Chapter 4
Effective Communication Skills in Negotiation

Prophetic Methods of Communication and Persuasion

Islamic rules on how to communicate effectively are a key part of building good business relationships with people of all races, countries, and faiths. Giving other people your thoughts, feelings, and sensations is what "communication" means.

Successful communication is crucial in negotiations as it facilitates people's finding common ground, expressing their needs, and seeing things from the other side's point of view. Excellent communication is very important for reaching a resolution in a disagreement, finalising a business deal, or making important choices. Communicating in a polite, clear, and concise way fosters collaboration and a pleasant atmosphere.

Dialogue is critical in negotiations as it enhances understanding between people with different goals, helps them understand each other, and keeps deals together. Talking to someone serves the dual purpose of finding out something or giving them information.

Misunderstandings can happen when someone can't clearly understand a question or piece of information. Clear and understandable information is useless if the person who receives it doesn't do something in return. The messenger knows that the message was received successfully when the receiver responds.

Communication is very important in talks because wants, thoughts, and plans all need to be shared. How well you can speak during talks may depend on achieving deals that are good for both sides in business deals, conflict resolution, and everyday interactions.

Sellers in the market must communicate, especially persuasively, to convince customers to purchase their goods. Muslims must uphold Islamic Shariah principles in all aspects of daily life, including conducting business wherever possible. Islam is the ideal religion for directing humankind's way of life since it's a comprehensive way of life.

> *"Allah says: 'This day I have perfected for you your religion and completed my favour upon you and have approved for you Islam as religion'" (Quran 5:3)*

In fact, this perfection encompasses all facets of life, including communication. The legacy of the Seerah illustrates how the Prophet (PBUH) disseminated his message through all accessible channels, including letters, in-person meetings, group discussions, and the dispatch of envoys.

Those who heard the Prophet Muhammad's (PBUH) words could understand them because he was always succinct, plain, and clear in his communication. The life of Prophet Muhammad (PBUH) is a real-world illustration of successful communication.

The following verse in the Holy Quran instructs followers on how to communicate effectively:

> *"Invite people to the way of your Lord with wisdom and beautiful preaching, and argue with them in ways that are best and most gracious." (Quran 16:125)*

When speaking with others, a person should remember key points, such as making eye contact, speaking clearly, being unique in tone, acting empathetically, and so forth.

Undoubtedly, all of these are effective ways to share one's thoughts, but the greatest source of motivation for Muslims in this regard is the Holy Prophet's (PBUH) Sunnah. It's essential to look at how people communicate in Islamic societies and how it affects communication in global contexts.

Investigating interpersonal communication concepts from an Islamic perspective is essential since Islam is a holistic way of life that includes the teachings, beliefs, and wider values that regulate human existence. These fundamental sources—the Quran and Hadiths, in particular—are the solid foundation for Islamic interpersonal communication norms.

Additionally, Islamic ethics are essential for directing communication for a wide range of purposes and activities, from public communication to the sharing of religious teachings.

From an Islamic Perspective, several core communication ethics include:

- The Tauhid principle, which underscores the purpose and essential nature of developing communication.

- The idea of controlling affirmative information without influencing opinions.

- The principle that building trust requires truthfulness and refraining from lying.

These guidelines emphasise the value of moral communication techniques in the Islamic setting and their wider social ramifications.

Principles of Effective Communication

Only a man who understands the art of situational word and sentence usage and respects listeners can inspire and uplift others' thoughts and emotions.

> *The Holy Prophet (PBUH) says, "some speeches have a magical inspiration" (Sahih Muslim)*

For this reason, it's critical to monitor one's speech pattern and word choice. People want the company of this man with inspiring discussion qualities; his words resolve many issues, and numerous barriers are overcome without resorting to force. The essential tenets of good communication are as follows:

Gentle Voice and Low Tone:

Islam emphasises the value of manners and etiquette, and quiet music is one of them. When someone speaks in a harsh tone, the listener feels uncomfortable. Muslims are instructed to respond softly even if someone speaks harshly.

When sending Hazrat Musa and Hazrat Haroon (AS) to preach to the Pharaoh (the Egyptian pharaoh who professed to be a deity and whose intentions were known to Almighty Allah for rejecting the sermon), the Almighty deity gave them the following advice:

> *"And speak to him with gentle speech that perhaps he may be reminded or fear [Allah]." (Quran 20:44)*

Naturally, Allah endowed humans with the ability to adjust the volume of their voices to suit the needs of the moment. As a result, the appropriate voice volume should be chosen based on the audience size.

> *"And do not turn your cheek [in contempt] toward people and do not walk through the earth exultantly. Indeed, Allah does not like everyone self-deluded and boastful. And be moderate in your pace and lower your voice; indeed, the most disagreeable of sounds is the voice of donkeys." (Quran 31:18-19)*

Choosing the right words

Using appropriate words, phrases, and sentences is crucial for efficient communication because, without them, we would be unable to express our ideas and intentions clearly to others.

Some employ esoteric, uncommon, or archaic language to gratify their inner selves or to inspire others. Most of the time, the listener is unable to comprehend these words.

This circumstance has a detrimental effect and makes listeners disinterested in the conversation, which prevents the communication from accomplishing its intended goals.

The adage "think before you speak" illustrates the importance of choosing your words carefully. Put another way, our words and thoughts should work well together.

The choice of simple, understandable terms is praiseworthy. Hazrat Ali (RA) suggests speaking at the listener's mental level.

Steer clear of a one-sided communication approach

God endowed humans with a single tongue and two ears, reminding us to talk and listen in moderation. Thus, the smart ones usually advise listening to others and finishing the speech quickly and thoroughly.

When a speaker dominates the conversation and forbids others from joining, it's considered an unpleasant act of unilateral communication. In these situations, listeners and participants typically grow disinterested and bored. Similar to how this mindset fosters rivalry among opponents.

> *"When two men come to you seeking judgment, do not judge for the first until you have heard the statement of the other. Soon you will know how to judge."* (Sahih Al-Bukhari)

Islamic teachings on communication can bring about a nonviolent and peaceful world. We see in daily life that good communication creates a pleasant atmosphere and reduces the likelihood of disagreements and confrontations.

Conversely, poor communication shatters harmony and breeds hostilities. The Islamic faith offered comprehensive direction and counsel before the modern world recognised the need for efficient communication.

The Prophet's (PBUH) Way of Listening

The Prophet (PBUH) had a lovely way of using the act of listening to make others feel valued. When he listened to others, he (PBUH) was focused and reverent, and he would show tremendous concern for everyone with whom he came into contact. The foundation of the Prophet's (PBUH) ability to listen was his pursuit of disseminating the Islamic message to mankind.

Allah Al-Mighty said:

> *"It was by a mercy from Allah that you were gentle with them. Had you been coarse and hard-hearted, they would have scattered from around you." (Quran 3:159)*

Building successful relationships requires effective communication because it's a two-way street; what is said must also be heard. Many of us have experienced situations where poor communication caused our relationships with significant others to deteriorate; either way, we felt misunderstood, or they felt ignored.

There are three components to the art of listening:

- Contribution (what is expressed)

- Procedure (hearing what is being said and considering it)

- Output (response, either spoken or unspoken)

It was Prophet Muhammad (PBUH) who exhibited the best communication abilities. He was the epitome of what it means to listen well. Here are some ways he showcased this:

The Prophet (PBUH) always gave his full attention to the person speaking to him. He would tilt both his head and torso toward the speaker, signalling that he valued what they were saying. This gesture made the speaker feel significant, building a bond between them that facilitated meaningful conversation.

Body language plays a crucial role in communication. Alongside keeping eye contact, a person's body language—such as hand gestures, facial emotions, and other movements—shows they are engaged in the conversation. Positive nonverbal cues like smiling, clasping hands, and nodding in agreement were evident in the Prophet's (PBUH) interactions, showcasing his remarkable communication skills.

Keeping eye contact when speaking with someone, especially of the same gender, is essential to communicate effectively. It signals to the speaker that they are being heard and respected. If eye contact is avoided or fixed on anything else, merely facing the speaker is insufficient. Such avoidant behaviour can hinder communication and convey a lack of focus, undermining the interaction.

The Prophet (PBUH) listened carefully, demonstrating through his actions that he felt what the speaker was going through and understood and believed what was being spoken. He avoided offering any quick fixes or judgments while doing this. Adopting such an attitude benefits the speaker therapeutically. One feels love, support, and no judgment.

Furthermore, one must make a genuine effort to see things from the other person's perspective and comprehend what they are trying to say.

The counselling profession uses a lot of empathy. Empathy is not the same as agreeing with the other person; it's the ability to recognise and comprehend their feelings and experiences. It takes compassion to adopt this mindset. People see the same circumstance differently, which must be acknowledged.

An effective listener like the Prophet (PBUH) attentively hears what's being said without interjecting. To be an effective listener, one must master this skill. When a speech is cut short, the speaker may become irritated, believing their words are unimportant or not being taken seriously.

The Prophet (PBUH) demonstrated patience in listening, allowing speakers the opportunity to completely express themselves before interjecting. He would inquire whether they had expressed what they wanted to say before answering, except in cases when he knew they were lying when he would intervene.

Whatever the gender, age, or belief, the Prophet (PBUH) was open to receiving advice. He sought counsel from his companions and wives on significant issues. Despite being the wisest man alive, he respected the wisdom of others and asked for their counsel, empowering his council with a sense of worth and accountability.

Similarly, his friends would voice their opinions, and he would always listen. The ability to hear wasn't impeded by age or experience. During challenging times, such as when Ali (RA) was asked for counsel regarding Aisha (RA) in the Ifk (slander) episode, the Prophet (PBUH) listened to him calmly, even though the advice he was given was harsh.

> "Oh Ali, if two people come to ask you to judge between them, do not judge in favour of the first, until you hear the word of the second, in order that you may know how to judge," the Prophet (PBUH) is reported to have said (Musnad Ahmad)

A just decision can only be reached by listening with wisdom.

> Prophet Muhammad (PBUH) is reported to have said to Ali (RA): "Oh Ali, if two people come to ask you to judge between them, do not judge in favour of the first until you hear the word of the second, in order that you may know how to judge." (Musnad Ahmad)

All this information highlights the exceptional listening skills of Prophet Muhammad (PBUH), emphasising how his attentive and compassionate listening made others feel valued and respected.

Prophet Muhammad (PBUH) is portrayed as the epitome of effective listening, setting an example for building successful relationships through compassionate and attentive communication.

Teaching Strategies of Prophet Muhammad (PBUH)

Allah selected the Prophet Muhammad (PBUH) to impart wisdom to humanity and eradicate ignorance. He was sent to instruct and serve as an example for his followers, an embodiment of a great teacher. As such, we ought to take cues from him and study his methods of instruction.

Prophet Muhammad's (PBUH) primary source of knowledge was divine revelation. His lessons were intended for the full individual and life. He imparted lessons about Islam, daily living, and labour. His lessons are timeless and transcend space and time. They imitate the fundamental components of curiosity, motivation, leadership, a step-by-step approach to learning, and learner-centricity.

Prophet Muhammad (PBUH) made his teachings memorable and practical by employing efficient teaching techniques. Because of his engaging and effective teaching methods, his students retained his lessons and changed their behaviour. Here are a few of his pedagogical techniques.

Prophet Muhammad (PBUH) always set an example for his people by practising what he preached using real-life events. He also used information to share personal experiences to emphasise the value of information and make it simpler for everyone to apply it daily.

He is the ideal example for everyone to aspire to be like.

> "There has certainly been for you in the Messenger of Allah an excellent pattern for anyone whose hope is in Allah and the Last Day and [who] remembers Allah often." (Quran, 33:21)

As a result, both before and after his passing, the Prophet Muhammad (PBUH) served as a mentor and an example of behaviour through his ideas, emotions, actions, speech, and life experiences. He could impart knowledge to his followers and associates by his deeds.

Employing the Narrative Technique

The Prophet (PBUH) would instruct his companions with stories. Narrating stories is a powerful tool for drawing in listeners and holding their interest while presenting lessons in a more approachable and useful way.

> *For instance, the Prophet (PBUH) said, "A man encountered a well while travelling and became extremely thirsty." After slaked his thirst, he descended the well and emerged. In the meantime, he noticed a panting, extremely thirsty dog slurping mud. "This dog is as thirsty as I am," he thought to himself. Thus, he descended the well once more and moistened his shoe with water. He did that, and Allah was pleased with him and pardoned him." (Sahih Al-Bukhari)*

Prophet Muhammad (PBUH) employed storytelling, particularly the narrative of the man, to impart the message of kindness toward animals.

Narratives are powerful tools because they create memorable lessons that stick in people's minds.

Making Use of Examples and Analogies

Prophet Muhammad (PBUH) stimulated listeners' creativity and curiosity by using analogies and examples to help them comprehend their faith on a deeper level. These analogies and examples were instrumental in streamlining and enhancing the listeners' comprehension of the ideas.

As an illustration,

> *"Would you notice any dirt on him if there was a river at your door and he took a bath in it five times a day?"* the Prophet (PBUH) posed this question to his followers. *"Not a trace of dirt would be left,"* they declared. *"That is the example of the five prayers with which Allah blots out (annuls) evil deeds,"* (Sahih Al-Bukhari)

Rather than merely communicating Allah's command and its advantages, the Prophet (PBUH) compared daily prayer to a bath. Praying five times a day also purifies one, like taking five baths a day would leave one clean. This made it easier for the populace to comprehend the advantages and significance of praying.

Prophet Muhammad (PBUH) was a superb educator and exemplary figure. His mission was to take the message of Allah to every human being on the planet. His instruction was explicit, to the point, and devoid of any room for ambiguity or mistake. As a result, his instructional techniques continue to be relevant and motivating.

Among his teaching techniques were questions, storytelling techniques, visuals, experiences, analogies, queries, and setting himself up as an example. By utilising all of these techniques, he created teachings that were powerful, remembered, and had a significant impact on the student's behaviour. This makes him an inspirational role model for educators across generations.

In essence, Prophet Muhammad (PBUH) exemplified the qualities of an exceptional educator, using effective teaching methods to impart wisdom and ensure lasting lessons. His teaching methods are relevant not only in religious contexts but can also be applied effectively in business negotiations. His approach to imparting wisdom and creating lasting impacts can offer valuable insights for modern business dealings.

Nonverbal Communication and Body Language in Negotiation

The point of a discussion is to reach an agreement that works for everyone, even if different people want different things. The spoken word is integral to getting what we wish to get across, but nonverbal speech is just as important in negotiations and is often ignored. Both spoken and unspoken words play a significant role in communicating meaning and helping people understand, showing that people choose how they want to communicate.

Many times, how well you negotiate depends on how well you prepare. A good negotiator will learn about the other side's goals long before they even enter the discussion room. However, a good mediator will also consider how body language and cultural differences affect the conversation.

When negotiating, reading body language is very important because it can tell if the other person is interested or open to your points of view. Body language can greatly affect how a negotiation goes, both during the discussion and before it starts. There are many kinds of body language, such as stance, hand movements, and facial expressions. They can be used to get better results if you understand how to use them properly.

If you watch the other person's body language, you can figure out what they think and how they feel about the discussion. Being able to spot these signs will help you change how you negotiate.

Principles of Effective Non-Verbal Communication

We can't escape nonverbal communication in our daily lives, but we should use caution while utilising the numerous gestures that make a conversation productive, long-lasting, and easily comprehended. It's estimated that nonverbal cues and signals account for two-thirds of our everyday communication.

For instance, when comparing listening to two people – one speaking on a mobile phone and the other directly in front of us – we typically grasp the second person's message better than the first. This is because we can observe their gestures and body language in addition to their words. Important guidelines for nonverbal communication have been expanded upon in the following sections.

Appropriate hand gestures can enhance communication by accurately conveying the context of the discussion. However, speakers should exercise caution when using their hands to avoid conveying unintended emotional intensity through hand movements. In the past, hand gestures, including pointing, held significant cultural and symbolic meanings, often associated with weapons.

> *The Holy Prophet Muhammad (PBUH) admonished against the act of pointing weapons at fellow Muslims, stating: "None of you should point out towards his Muslim brother with a weapon, for he does not know, Satan (Devil) may tempt him to hit him and thus he would fall into a pit of (Hell) fire." (Sahih Muslim)*

Being cheerful is regarded as a virtuous deed that the All-Powerful Allah rewards. Conversely, dull expressions also arise when one encounters someone undesired. A person's facial expressions reveal something about their inner sentiments. As a result, when chatting with someone, one should make nice facial gestures to send a positive message of warmth and affection. In general, happiness manifests on a person's face after meeting them.

The Holy Prophet Muhammad (PBUH) emphasised the significance of even the smallest acts of goodness, stating:

> *"Do not consider any act of goodness as being insignificant, even if it is meeting your brother with a cheerful face." (Sahih Muslim)*

> *In another hadith, the Prophet (PBUH) declared that meeting a brother with a smile is an act of charity. (Tirmidhi)*

Thus, cheerfulness is regarded as an act of goodness deserving of reward from Almighty Allah.

Our body organs significantly influence our everyday conversations. The eyes are one of these organs used to perceive different emotions. We should use caution while using our eyes in speech, as they can send messages of love, rage, envy, approval, and disapproval. The saying "eyes also speak" is well recognised since eyes are a very effective way to communicate our inner feelings.

> *In the incident of the "Conquest of Mecca," when the companions of the Prophet Muhammad (PBUH) expressed a desire for him to use a subtle gesture, such as blinking, to eliminate a potential threat during the*

> *ceremony of allegiance, the Prophet (PBUH) responded by saying: "It is not fitting for a Prophet to engage in deceitful manoeuvres with his eyes." (Sahih Al-Bukhari)*

This response reflects the Prophet's adherence to honesty and integrity in all his actions, even in moments of potential danger or conflict. It's vital to avoid giving someone the wrong impression by continuously staring at them. Generally speaking, when someone speaks, and the audience disregards them, the speaker becomes upset because they gauge attentiveness through eye contact. Therefore, we should look directly at the audience when conveying a message.

Advice for Interpreting Body Language Correctly

You should pay close attention to three main body language cues during a negotiation: posture, hand movements, and facial expressions. Of course, this is just the beginning; there's much more to it.

First, let's start with facial expressions. A sincere smile conveys happiness or satisfaction, whereas a forced or tense smile may indicate attempts to conceal unfavourable emotions. Similarly, a furrowed brow denotes uncertainty or worry, while lifted eyebrows can signal surprise or interest.

Another useful body language indicator is hand gestures. Hand gestures can sometimes be significantly more successful than spoken communication. Several telltale indicators of discomfort, including tapping, fidgeting, and anxiousness, should be noted. Conversely, open hands convey sincerity, integrity, and confidence.

Posture is another important factor. Sitting or standing upright exudes strength, focus, and confidence. Conversely, slouching or leaning conveys a lack of attention, engagement, frailty, and disinterest.

In negotiations, body language is extremely important, and deciphering it requires an acute sense of observation and interpretation. This ability can help uncover concealed signs, hone bargaining tactics, and concede good communication at critical times. The advice provided here will give you a competitive edge in negotiating future negotiations successfully and effectively.

Chapter 5
Conflict Resolution and Mediation

Prophetic Approaches to Resolving Conflicts

For those who practice it, Islam is a comprehensive way of life (*Deen*) that offers guidance on all aspects of life, including handling conflict. When religion is viewed as a way of life, it suggests an integrated way of living that incorporates both personal and professional life via Islamic faith and theology (*Iman*).

As a result, all disagreements in Islamic work ethics must be evaluated in light of the Quran and Sunnah teachings.

Islamic-based dispute resolution, which has its roots in the Quran and hadith, places a high value on settling disputes by techniques like *Tahkim* (arbitration) as well as *Sulh* (mediation), which aligns with the values of compassion, justice, and reconciliation.

This approach promotes a diverse legal landscape within different schools of jurisprudence, fostering peaceful conflict resolution in line with Islamic values.

It draws inspiration from the divine revelation in the Quran and the teachings of the Prophet Muhammad (PBUH). Let's look at these aspects and Prophetic approaches to this matter.

Strategies for Peaceful Resolution of Disputes in Accordance with Islamic Teachings

Conflict management principles have been discussed in the Quran in general and in specific contexts that account for religious and cultural differences and promote conflict resolution.

Institutions of dispute settlement have existed for as long as humans have. Humans are endowed with both benefits and drawbacks, which can occasionally lead to disagreement or conflict with other people, their surroundings, and themselves.

When they encounter issues or disagreements, they instinctively seek a way to resolve the conflict. Furthermore, as human civilisation advances, so do conflicts and the means of resolving them.

The Quran clarifies that disagreements and conflicts that arise in daily life are inevitable. Since humans are endowed with the capacity for cognition and revelation in organising their lives, they must resolve disputes as his khalifa on this planet.

The Quran instructs Muslims to refer to its Prophetic traditions to settle conflicts. It offers clear guidance on handling and resolving disputes with a prescribed hierarchy.

The Quran discusses conflict management concepts both generally and in particular settings that consider cultural and religious diversity and encourage dispute resolution.

Key concepts for preventing conflict and resolving it through negotiating can be derived from the teachings of the Quran.

Investigating Before Acting on What We Hear

In the Quran, Allah says:

> *"Believers, if an evildoer brings you news, ascertain the correctness of the report fully, lest you unwittingly harm others, and then regret what you have done." (Quran 49:6)*

People frequently become agitated and turn to violence based just on gossip and rumours without checking the accuracy of what they have been told. Sometimes, they hear wholly untrue things, but by the moment they understand this, it's too late—they have already turned to violence, which has caused several casualties and destruction of property.

Defusing the situation

How do you diffuse a scenario if you're negotiating and there's unrest, confusion, or anything else that makes you feel anxious? It's crucial to have the ability to change the direction of a nervous discussion and to have it in your negotiation toolbox. Knowing the solution to the question of how to diffuse tense discussions allows you to assess your own level of self-awareness. Prior to engaging in a discussion, identify the circumstances that could enrage you. Be ready to implement the solutions you have created, detailing how you will handle such circumstances throughout the negotiation.

Call a "time out" and leave the negotiation table if you find yourself "losing your cool" in the face of an unexpected circumstance during the negotiation. Keep your distance until you have regained composure both mentally and physically.

NEGOTIATING WITH FAITH

The Quran tells us to avoid retaliating when someone provokes us and to instead diffuse the issue.

> *"Whenever they kindle the fire of war, God puts it out."*
> *(Quran, 5:64)*

This line, "God puts it [the fire of violence] out," suggests that rather than responding to the provocation by engaging in combat, we should employ the wisdom God has given us in the form of patience and avoidance to restore peace. Muslims' response to provocation will be like water on the flames of conflict and violence if they choose to follow the path of *Sabr* (patience) and avoidance.

Alternatively, Muslims will only fan the flames if they respond to the provocation with violence. The Quran has numerous verses that encourage Muslims to practice avoidance and *Sabr*. Muslims would destroy the fundamental causes of inter-communal violence if they used this Quranic technique for situational defusing.

The necessity of refraining from naive bias and provocations

The Quran recounts that during the Treaty of Hudaybiya, when the Prophet's adversaries displayed bigotry toward Muslims, the Muslims did not reciprocate. Instead, they continued to be firmly grounded in God-awareness. The Treaty of Hudaybiya became possible because the believers behaved differently than their opponents. This pact was described by God as a "clear victory." Exactly two years after this contract was made, Islam conquered all of Arabia.

Muslims' history would suddenly take a different course if they lived by the above-mentioned Quranic verse. Additionally, it would completely eradicate intergroup violence. Community riots frequently occur as a result of Muslims' uniform response to the discriminatory actions of others. This intensifies the argument and eventually sparks rioting.

When Muslims have been provoked by others, they have often responded with similar bias. However, their response would have been very different if they had followed the guidance of the Quran. This adherence could have saved many lives.

> As the Quran says, "The good deed and the evil deed are not equal. Repel [evil] by that [deed] which is better; and thereupon the one whom between you and him is enmity [will become] as though he was a devoted friend." (Quran 41:34)

> The Prophet Muhammad (PBUH) also related that "Evil cannot be wiped out through evil. Rather, evil can be wiped out only through goodness." (Musnad Ahmad)

This hadith expresses a heavenly principle. The idea that virtue alone is how all evil can be eradicated governs the entire globe. Evil would have taken over the entire planet if that were not the case. Muslims nowadays are seeking to put a stop to evil by turning to evil themselves, which is contrary to what Islam teaches.

They wish to stop provocation with provocation, hate with hate, enmity with enmity, and prejudice with communal prejudice. This whole thing goes against the laws of heaven and is doomed to fail. Muslims who insist on carrying on in this fashion will have to create an imagined universe that suits them, as they can't possibly succeed in the actual world in this way.

The Prophet's Example

In the context of conflict resolution, negotiation is a conversation between parties to resolve disagreements and come to a mutually beneficial agreement. It's an effective dispute resolution technique that calls for expertise and training.

The exchange of information and understanding is the basis for diplomatic negotiation. The three fundamental strategies are persuasion, concession, and negotiation. The most tangible form of negotiation is compromise, which the Prophet of Islam made possible in the Treaty of Hudaybiya to reach an understanding of the desires of both Muslims and Quraysh.

The Quraysh of Mecca planned for battle, and Khalid bin Walid—who would go on to become one of Islam's generals organised all the Makkan tribes to oppose Medina pilgrims. When the Prophet (PBUH) learned of the Meccans' intentions, he promptly sent out a message stating he had come for the pilgrimage, not for the war.

Despite initial rejection of the Prophet's message, the ancient Quraysh chieftain Urwa stepped in with a peace initiative, approaching the Prophet (PBUH) to negotiate.

The Prophet (PBUH) dispatched an agent to Quraysh, but they killed the camel he was riding on with the message. He, however, never intended for war to occur at this time, and the conversation with Urwa remained unsatisfactory. Even when the Quraysh decisively disproved the faith, the Prophet (PBUH) continued to advocate for peace and ongoing negotiations.

After much work, the Prophet dispatched a second envoy, his close colleague Uthman bin Affan, to resume the negotiations. Eventually, a compromise was reached and put in writing. The draught treaty presented a number of challenges, and in this delicate position, the Prophet (PBUH) showed perfect patience.

The text that was signed required the Prophet (PBUH) and Muslims to make many concessions; in fact, the Prophet (PBUH) had to remove the term "Apostle of Allah" from the document, a move that his companions found objectionable. Nevertheless, the Prophet expertly negotiated this compromise to prevent conflict.

Therefore, the Treaty of Hudaybiya is a profound example of conflict resolution and negotiation in Islamic history. It demonstrates the Prophet Muhammad's (PBUH) strategic diplomacy and commitment to peace. Rich in lessons, this event is often cited as a benchmark for effective negotiation and compromise.

Process of Alternative Dispute Resolution in Islamic Law

Instead of violent conflict resolution, Islam also supports peaceful conflict settlement. So, it's clear that alternative conflict resolution (ADR) is not against Islamic law. For more than 1400 years, Muslims have used alternative dispute settlement (ADR) to settle their disagreements without going to court. These ways are mentioned and supported by Islamic law authorities because Islam values peace over conflict and unity over discord.

In Islam, disagreements are settled by blending broad principles with clear laws and rules. The rules in this document are meant to set up a framework for dealing with disagreements. Alternative dispute settlement (ADR) methods and normal courts are deeply interconnected in Islamic culture.

It's believed that legal systems in countries that don't follow Islamic principles are less effective than those in countries that adopt traditional ways of resolving disputes.

People believe that the Prophet Muhammad (PBUH) was sent by Allah and is credited with founding Islam. He was a strong backer of peaceful conflict settlement and used these methods. In Islam, ADR is seen as religiously pure because it's based on the Quran and was supported by the Prophet (PBUH) while he was alive.

In Islam, alternative conflict settlement (ADR) is permissible as long as it adheres to the rules regarding what is allowed or not allowed in work.

After Abu Musa Al Ashri was made a qadi (judge), the second caliph of Islam, Muhammad bin Khattab, gave him a famous letter that talked about a lot of different ways to settle disagreements without violence. He could use this letter to help him make decisions about cases. In the Quran, it says,

> *"The believers are but a single brotherhood; so make peace and reconciliation (Sulh) between two (contending) brothers; and fear Allah, that ye may receive mercy." (Quran 49:10)*

However, modern perspectives increasingly recognise the significance of peaceful conflict resolution through arbitration, compromise, and mediation in Islamic justice. While many say Islam prioritises court cases for settling disputes, the Hadith and the Quran don't stress the necessity of legal proceedings as the primary means of resolution. Instead, they value talking things out, meditating, etc., more than standing up for legal rights.

Islamic ADR methods are discussed in the Quran. Some of these are *Tahkim* (arbitration), *Fatwa* (expert decision), *Med-arb* (a mix of Sulh and Tahkim), and *Muhtasib* (ombudsman). Sulh includes bargaining, settling disagreements, making peace, and deciding what to do.

Tahkim (Arbitration) has roots in pre-Islamic Arabia, where it served as a way to settle a wide range of social and business disagreements through justice.

Until the trial chief could make it so, an arbitration decision lacked enforceability unless all parties agreed to it. The people involved usually agreed that the decisions made by the judges chosen at the ukaz, a monthly Mecca fair, were legally binding. In cases where disputes can't be resolved or prevented, individuals can see help from judges under Islamic law.

The Quran, the Sunnah, the Ijma, and the Qiyas all back this up. It's very important to stress that under Islamic law, a mediator has the same power to settle conflicts and make decisions as a judge in a regular court.

In this way, an arbitrator's job is like that of a judge during the Islamic period. Still, arbitration can't solve all problems. For example, it can't solve problems with gifts, marriage, child custody, or divorce.

"To finish a dispute" (*Sulh*) can mean to negotiate, mediate, reconcile, or come to an agreement on what to do. It can be done alone or with the help of a neutral third party. Arbitration doesn't fall under Sulh because it's held under different rules. Action agreement, peace, mediation, and discussion are all things that Sulh talks about.

They can all be easily put into the group of alternative conflict resolution (ADR). What is great about Sulh is its flexibility and its three components: bargaining, mediation, and settlement.

Fatwa (Expert determination): Another way to settle a legal dispute is through a fatwa, which is another name for a legal opinion. In the Islamic faith, a fatwa is a religious rule made by an expert that is seen as a holy law. According to Islamic custom, a fatwa can only be issued by a recognised law expert, such as an ulama (a group of teachers) in Sunni schools or a mufti (a leader of the Shia schools). It's customary to give fatwas based on reason and logic (ijtihad). While the fatwa's findings are not officially binding, they are still good to follow. Many times in Islamic history, people have brought up difficult problems to Muftis, who then issued fatwas in response.

Med-arb (combination of *Sulh* and *Tahkim*): Med-arb, which combines Tahkim and Sulh, is another type of ADR utilised in Islam. In this method, the arbitrator begins by attempting mediation and negotiating with the parties to resolve the dispute. If mediation proves unsuccessful, the process proceeds to arbitration for a final decision. Islam views Medi-arb as a unique feature that blends the co-sensuality of the mediation process with the finality of arbitration. The entire dispute resolution process is divided into two phases: arbitration is utilised to provide finality to the process after mediation. This method's blended process and distinctive qualities set it apart from Sulh and Tahkim.

Ombudsman (*Muhtasib*): Since Allah delivered the Quran, Muslims have followed the ombudsman practice, as articulated in various verses of the Holy Quran. According to Islamic law, the main duty of the ombudsman (Muhtasib) is to take accounts (hisbah). The Muhstasib performed a variety of religious obligations, including praying (salat) and maintaining mosques.

Additionally, they regulated communal affairs and market behaviour, enforcing regulations regarding the accuracy of weights and measures and the sincerity of commercial transactions. City affairs also involve keeping streets and roads clean and well-lit at night and avoiding building factories or residences that would be in opposition to the neighbourhood's interests.

According to the analysis of the literature and practices indicated above, the manner in which justice is administered in any society can be used to gauge the social consciousness and knowledge of the general people. The parties can select from a range of alternative dispute resolution (ADR) methods, including fair justice according to Islamic principles.

However, social and political overtones have compromised the institution's credibility over time. In conclusion, extrajudicial conflict resolution is nothing new; all civilisations have long used natural, non-judicial methods of resolving disputes. According to the explanation above, Islamic principles of fair justice always allow the parties to choose from a variety of alternative dispute resolution procedures.

Role of Mediation and Arbitration in Islamic Law

Islam settles disputes by combining general principles with authoritative legal and regulatory frameworks. Along with being a major proponent of nonviolent dispute settlement, the Prophet Muhammad (PBUH) also put these methods into practice, which helped to establish Islam. There are a few different ways to settle conflicts: Arbitration, Conciliation, Mediation and Lok-Adalat.

A third party who is impartial and called a "Mediator" helps the parties work toward resolving their differences amicably; the neutral party doesn't make decisions on their behalf. Following mediation, the parties continue to have authority over the resolution.

Arbitration implies that arbitration can't occur without a valid agreement before a dispute develops. Parties submit their disapproval to one or more arbitrators in this way of resolving disputes. The decision made by the arbitrator, known as the "Award," is binding on the parties.

Conciliation refers to a non-binding procedure wherein the disputing parties seek the conciliator's assistance—an impartial third party—to reach a mutually acceptable resolution to their differences. Conciliation is a less formal type of arbitration.

Conversely, negotiation is an informal method in which the parties begin discussions with one another to reach a mutually acceptable resolution without the assistance of a third party.

Last but not least, Lok-Adalat is the name of an informal venue where disputes can be resolved without overemphasising legal subtleties and where talks can take place before a judge. The Lok-Adalat's final order is binding on all parties involved and will be regarded as a civil court decision. The parties are not entitled to an appeal of the Lok-Adalat's decision.

Utilising Third-Party Mediation to Facilitate Fair Settlements

Within Muslim culture, the idea of mediation is not new. It's generally accepted as the standard method of resolving conflicts in the Muslim community. Regardless of how they may practice their faith, Muslims are obligated to observe it both officially and culturally.

Islam places a high value on wassatah (mediation), a constructive dispute resolution process that uses a mediator— an impartial third party —to help the parties involved reach a mutually agreeable conclusion.

Other verses in the Holy Quran expressly support mediation. The Holy Quran demands mercy in defence situations and justice in revenge situations. The Prophet's (PBUH) Sunnah is quite clear regarding conflict settlement.

The Prophet (PBUH) engaged in mediation among Muslims and non-Muslims. The same custom was followed in the eras of the Prophet's (PBUH) companions.

The Prophet (PBUH) handled most of the community's problems through mediation and arbitration in Medina. Meccans have always respected the knowledge and intelligence of the Prophet (PBUH), and they called him al-amin because, in times of need, they would seek his advice to settle their differences and accept his judgment.

A disagreement between a lender and a borrower was settled by the Prophet (PBUH), who suggested that the creditor take half of the amount owed to him in exchange for the debtor making an immediate, full payment rather than making smaller payments over time.

How This Works:

The process has six steps in order, and each one is purposefully created to improve understanding, communication, and bargaining.

1. **First Client Intake (Set Up):** At this fundamental stage, the mediator has the first meeting to collect relevant facts regarding the conflict. This entails reviewing the documents, having one-on-one discussions with each side, and figuring out the main concerns. After evaluating the case, a committee makes recommendations regarding whether to move forward to the following meeting.

2. **Opening Session:** This is the official start of mediation. During this second stage, the mediator introduces the parties, explains their position, and sets ground rules essential to the process's seamless operation. The mediator can pinpoint the main concerns because all parties are given uninterrupted time to express their points of view.

3. **Joint Session:** During the third phase, the joint session gives

all sides a continuous forum to voice their opinions regarding the disagreement. To promote efficient communication, the mediator fosters a courteous and productive environment that facilitates the open expression of feelings, concerns, and points of view.

4. **Private One-on-One Sessions:** To speed up negotiations after joint sessions, the mediator may hold private sessions with each party. In an effort to discover common ground, these private sessions offer a safe space to address underlying issues and generate potential answers.

5. **Problem-solving and negotiation:** These activities are part of the fourth stage. Options are developed via various techniques, including mediator suggestions, discussion groups, and group processes. The mediator leads a brainstorming session to reach a mediated settlement that defuses the issue and lays the groundwork for future relationships.

6. **Conclusion and Agreement:** The goal of the last phase is to reach a mutually agreeable conclusion. If the mediation is successful, the mediator helps draft a written agreement that details the agreed-upon provisions. The parties' signatures on this document give it legal validity and create a legally binding contract that ends the mediation procedure. A mediator fulfils two primary duties in resolving conflict. First and foremost, they urge the parties to settle in a way that will result in a fair resolution. Second, they must remain impartial and empower the parties to make their own decisions. Islam recognises and acknowledges the limitations imposed by the law; however, Islamic law explicitly permits mediation.

Mediation needs to be healthy and legal. An agreement's subject matter can't conflict with Islamic law or values. A mediator fulfils two primary duties in resolving conflict. First and foremost, the mediator urges the parties to mediate in a way that will result in a fair resolution. Second, the decision-making authority should remain with the parties involved in the disagreement and the mediator.

The Holy Quran doesn't mention the credentials, the process of choosing a mediator, or how the mediator helps parties settle their differences in a disagreement. As long as they are acknowledged for what they are and don't violate any Islamic legal precepts, anyone, regardless of approach, may serve as an Islamic mediator.

The reliability of arbitration and mediation is significantly influenced by the arbiter's abilities. In Islam, great emphasis is placed on justice and honesty in a mediator. This is clearly articulated in the letter Imam Ali wrote to Malik al-Ashtar. The Holy Quran also underscores this principle:

> "O ye who believe! Be steadfast witnesses for Allah in equity, and let not hatred of any people seduce you that ye deal not justly. Deal justly that is nearer to your duty. Observe your duty to Allah. Lo! Allah is informed of what ye do." (Quran 5:8)

> Moreover, it advises, "Be firm in standing for justice, even against yourselves or your parents and relatives, whether they are rich or poor. Allah is more worthy of both." (Quran 4:135)

Upholding Principles of Justice and Equity in Dispute Resolution

Fostering fairness and mutual respect during talks depends on upholding the ideals of justice and equity in dispute settlement. This entails ensuring that each party has an equal chance to voice its opinions and concerns. To preserve the integrity of the process, negotiators must actively listen, maintain objectivity, and refrain from prejudice. Communication and decision-making must be transparent to foster accountability and confidence.

Furthermore, fair treatment calls for considering the particular requirements and circumstances of every party instead of using a one-size-fits-all strategy. By supporting less powerful parties to make sure their perspectives are heard, mediators should work to maintain a balance in the dynamics of power. Ultimately, the objective is to come to a decision that is agreeable to all parties and consistent with more general notions of justice and fairness, fostering enduring peace and collaboration.

Chapter 6
Negotiation Tactics and Strategies

Mastering the Art of Negotiation

In Islam, where dealings are governed by rules that comply with Shariah law, the ability to negotiate is essential. Professionals in the field need to be able to handle these negotiations properly. Whether you work in insurance, investments, Islamic banking, or any business, developing your negotiating skills can result in more fair and advantageous agreements. Let's examine some essential advice for improving your negotiating abilities in relation to the Islamic context.

In preparing for negotiations within the Islamic framework, it's crucial for you to grasp the tenets of the Islamic worldview. Before you engage in any kind of negotiation, grasp the ethical and religious concepts that steer Shariah-compliant transactions. This understanding will ensure that you can handle discussions with ease and uphold Islamic values in the process.

Your success in negotiations hinges on preparation. Before starting any conversations, do extensive research on the parties involved, the state of the market, and the particulars of the transaction. Knowing each party's objectives and demands will help you create recommendations that meet everyone's interests while adhering to the principles of Islamic financing.

In Islam, trust and relationships are essential for fruitful talks. Building long-lasting trust with other parties is essential to successful commercial partnerships. Make integrity, open communication, and openness your top priorities. Exhibiting a dedication to moral behaviour cultivates confidence and establishes the foundation for discussions based on shared dignity.

In talks, listening is a skill that is frequently underutilised. By actively listening, you can discern your counterparts' worries, priorities, and deeper reasons. Armed with this knowledge, you can modify your offers to suit their requirements while adhering to Shariah law. Negotiations become more collaborative when you show respect and know other people's viewpoints.

Negotiations need persistence and patience, especially when dealing with complicated financial transactions. Shariah law mandates strict adherence, and negotiation in this realm often involves complex systems. Throughout the bargaining process, remain calm and patient and be ready for lengthy conversations. This mindset fosters a good environment and encourages fruitful conversation.

Negotiations typically involve cultural diversity. Understanding the subtleties of expectations, decision-making processes, and communication styles requires a high level of cultural sensitivity. Effective negotiations thrive when participants embrace and respect these cultural differences.

Your primary goal in negotiations should be to achieve fair and advantageous agreements for both parties. Aim for win-win outcomes that benefit all parties involved and are consistent with Islamic beliefs. This strategy builds enduring business partnerships while still upholding Islam's moral cornerstone.

Gaining proficiency in the art of negotiating requires a variety of skills, including a dedication to ethical behaviour, knowledge of the rules of Shariah, and good communication. Commercial transaction professionals can negotiate with courage and integrity by prioritising win-win solutions, actively listening, rigorous preparation, and trust.

The ability to negotiate effectively will continue to grow in importance as industries evolve, fostering long-lasting, ethical commercial partnerships that adhere to Islamic finance norms.

Procedure of Bargaining in Islam

In Islamic finance, adherence to specific protocols is crucial for buying or selling transactions. These protocols include:

- **Intent to Purchase:** A genuine intention to purchase is essential. If you lack this intention, abstain from bidding and promptly cancel any price agreements to avoid inconveniencing or harming the seller, particularly if the buyer's actions prolong negotiations unnecessarily.

- **Completion of Agreements**: Once parties reach an agreement, honouring and concluding the sale and purchase transaction is imperative to avoid disappointing the seller.

- **Respect for Others' Offers:** Refrain from bidding on items already offered by someone else.

- **Avoidance of Envy:** Don't harbour envy towards others involved in the transaction.

- **Refrain from Negative Remarks:** Avoid discussing or highlighting others' shortcomings.

- **Abstain from Hatred:** It's crucial not to harbour feelings of hatred towards others involved.

- **Conflict Avoidance:** Strive to prevent conflicts or disputes.

- **Fair Bidding:** Don't engage in placing higher bids on offers made by others.

- **Moderate Praise for Goods:** Sellers should avoid excessive praise of their goods.

- **Abstain from Complaints:** Customers should refrain from complaining about the goods.

Furthermore, it's crucial to note that bidding on offers made by others, especially when a seller is negotiating with a potential buyer, may lead to potential conflicts or animosity among vendors. Islam emphasises the importance of maintaining harmony and avoiding conflicts in transactions. Any discord among sellers can adversely affect their performance and business progress. The Prophet (PBUH) emphasises the importance of respecting fellow Muslims and refraining from betrayal, deception, lying, or humiliation. Taqwā, or God-consciousness, lies in upholding these principles. It is prohibited for a Muslim to harm, seize goods, or defame fellow Muslims.

Ethics of Bargaining in Islam

In the Hadith records, Islam offers guidelines for bargaining ethics that don't give rise to the presence of the aggrieved party:

> *The Prophet (PBUH) said: "Let no one sell on his brother's sale," according to Ibn 'Umar. It is not appropriate for someone to preach or apply their brother's sermon without authorisation. (Muslim)*

> *According to Ibn 'Umar, the Prophet Muhammad (PBUH) commanded, "Let no one of you bid for his brother's offer." (Sahih Al-Bukhari)*

Bidding on regular sales is one of the many things that people involved in the trade always do. It's clear that the seller wants the goods to sell for a high price, and the buyer wants to buy at a low price. This is why buying (on goods that don't have a set price) is usually linked to setting prices. People who want to buy or sell things must deal with each other to set prices.

The hadith mentioned highlights ethical considerations that apply to transactions involving both parties. It prohibits bidding on or purchasing from someone else's offer, a rule that applies to both the seller and the buyer.

Sellers engaging in unethical practices may offer goods at a lower price to customers already negotiating with other vendors or provide higher quality goods at the same price. The aim is to sway potential customers to choose their goods over those of competitors. However, seizing potential customers through deceit is highly unethical and thus forbidden.

Potential purchasers engaging in bidding on someone else's offer, contrary to the ethics outlined in the hadith, can manifest in various scenarios:

1. In an ongoing bidding process or past purchasing and selling transactions, the second potential buyer offers a higher price than the first.

2. The second potential buyer, pledging to buy at a higher price, persuades the previous seller to cancel the sale with the first buyer.

3. Actively placing a bid on another buyer's offer when the new bidder announces a shortage of the items the previous buyer bid for.

This technique ensures the second buyer secures the item while preventing the first bidder from doing so.

The prohibition in the hadith underscores that undue competition among potential buyers is unjustified in transactions involving the exchange of goods. The Prophet carefully addresses this issue, emphasising that even if a buyer is genuinely interested in an item offered by someone else, they may only bid on products not currently sought after.

This prohibition protects vulnerable individuals by preventing those with greater socioeconomic means from unfairly leveraging their position over those with less. Another hadith allows bidding on items not already claimed; bidding on the items becomes permissible if the initial bidder has left the transaction site.

In essence, bidding on items offered by other potential buyers or proposing the termination of an existing sale with promises of higher prices is not permitted. Offers can only be made while both potential buyers and sellers are actively engaged in the bidding process, as straying from this guideline may lead to conflict or hostility between buyers.

Similarly, sellers may also engage in bidding on offers made by others. For example, while negotiating with potential customer A, another seller might offer the same item to A at a lower price or provide higher-quality items at the same price.

Sellers are advised against proceeding if the item they wish to buy or sell is already up for bid or has been previously sold, as this could lead to potential disputes or animosity between vendors.

Islam protects this, ensuring that any transactions will not become a point of conflict for the people concerned. Enmity amongst other sellers will impact each other's performance, particularly for sellers. Don't worry about the company's success; the animosity will lead to other negative outcomes.

The hadith under discussion is contained in a lengthy collection of hadiths; the guidelines governing the morality of this offer are complemented by the restriction on accepting another applicant's proposal until the initial applicant chooses not to pursue a relationship. The same principle underlies the prohibition: those who arrive later must consider the morality of fair competition. Don't take under false pretences, having the meaning of the latter party in mind. In terms of the law of sale and buy, there's a difference in revenue if there's a sale and purchase using this forbidden bidding method, specifically:

1) Jumhur says that purchasing and selling are both permissible and immoral.

2) Ibn Hazm and Hanafiyah both claimed that buying and selling was forbidden in one of their histories.

Diverse perspectives on the validity and ethics of buying and selling transactions often stem from differing interpretations of the pillars of lawful and illegitimate commerce. For the fuqaha, who emphasise adherence to the pillars' requirements, both purchasing and selling are deemed permissible yet subject to moral considerations. However, some contest the validity of buying and selling laws, citing perceived incompleteness in certain hadiths.

In transactions involving buying and selling, bargaining is inherent, with each party bearing ethical responsibilities, especially during negotiations. In Islam, haggling is permissible as long as it doesn't cause harm to any participant. Any agreement that proves detrimental to one party and contravenes ethical principles is deemed void throughout the transaction. It's imperative in the Islamic economic framework that all practices are rooted in the teachings of the Sunnah and the Quran.

Overcoming Obstacles and Dealing with Difficult Negotiators

The goal of negotiation is to arrive at a win-win solution that includes requirements, rewards, and concessions. Negotiators often find this delicate balance between firms and professionals difficult to achieve, even with their extensive experience. What obstacles exist for negotiating, then?

A constructive negotiating skills training course foundation knows the answer to this question since it enables you to identify potential roadblocks and get past them. Let's have a look at what Islamic teachings guide us in this situation. In the Quran, Allah says:

> *"And the servants of the Gracious God are those who walk on the earth in a dignified manner, and when the ignorant address them, they say, 'Peace!'" (Quran, 25: 64)*

Speaking softly to others and sincerely trying to persuade them is one of the most effective strategies to win Allah's love when faced with challenging conduct.

Furthermore, the Holy Quran tells us to control our anger:

> *"And those who suppress anger and pardon others."*
> *(Quran, 3:135)*

Sometimes, other people's behaviour makes our blood boil, and we react violently. We want to let them know how we feel, believing that a firm confrontation will stop their actions. Rather, we just make things worse by letting their venom fester inside of us and fuelling even more rage.

> *The Prophet Muhammad (PBUH) said, "The strong person is not the one who throws his adversaries to the ground. The strong person is the one who contains himself when he is angry." (Sahih Al-Bukhari)*

When the Prophet (PBUH) faced difficulties, he followed these two steps:

- Pray to Allah and put your trust in Him.

- Consult with his reliable confidantes for advice.

But his process's sequence remained constant. A person's initial reaction to an occurrence can reveal a lot about their attitude and comprehension. The Prophet (PBUH), for example, always chose to turn to the Creator in prayer prior to consulting His creation.

In Islamic tradition, overcoming obstacles and dealing with difficult negotiators is grounded in principles derived from the Quran and the teachings of the Prophet Muhammad (PBUH). These principles emphasise patience, wisdom, fairness, and a strong ethical foundation.

There are situations in which facing up to a challenging negotiation can be almost as difficult as having a discussion. Being ready for these talks in advance will make you feel more capable of handling them.

Dealing with challenging individuals is unavoidable, especially if your profession necessitates negotiating. Even though you cannot completely avoid them, there are several strategies you can use to effectively negotiate with challenging individuals. Here are some further Islamic strategies and principles to navigate such situations:

Taking on difficult negotiating techniques frequently calls for rude or combative actions. It's critical to keep parties away from the issue. Keep your focus on the matters at hand to refocus conversations on the real issues at hand and steer clear of personal conflicts.

React assertively but diplomatically to personal insults, making an effort to comprehend the underlying issues. Empathic responses have the power to reduce tension and create a productive negotiation atmosphere.

Make an effort to understand the other party's intentions at every stage of the negotiation process. Make sure all parties are aware of each other's goals and points of view by asking information-seeking questions, providing summaries, and communicating clearly.

Many people who are challenging to work with in a negotiating situation have strong opinions, are aware of their abilities, and feel that their efforts should be acknowledged. While those things are not always negative, they can make talks difficult. When presenting your own thoughts in these situations, do it with confidence. When the other person pushes back, equal their strength with your own and don't back down or back down. That kind of approach will be met with a lot of dominating people who enjoy the display of power.

When confronted with difficult strategies, keep an open mind and look for creative answers. Look for options that satisfy the needs of both sides. Being adaptable encourages cooperation, which raises the possibility of coming up with win-win solutions. Developing a relationship fosters collaboration. Establish common objectives and take an active part in problem-solving dialogues to facilitate fruitful interactions. Use objective standards such as market value to ground conversations in justice and lessen the need for challenging strategies.

The management of negotiation dynamics is aided by emotional intelligence. Challenging strategies can try to provoke feelings; keeping emotional intelligence enables one to judge motives and reacts accordingly. It makes it possible to approach talks with composure, basing choices on reasoned analysis rather than gut feelings.

Keeping your cool and emotional quotient up is essential while handling challenging negotiation strategies. Even when faced with difficult emotions, maintain your composure and rationality throughout. It might be detrimental to judgment to let feelings guide one's actions. By identifying and controlling your emotions while upholding a professional manner, you can demonstrate emotional intelligence. When negotiating, it's essential to actively listen in order to understand the concerns and objectives of the opposing party.

Inform them of the repercussions: If all other methods have failed, this may be a useful tactic. Make sure the person knows what will happen if they don't want to compromise or if you're trying to negotiate with them and they are stubborn. They may be more inclined to make concessions to meet everyone's needs if they realise that their failure to cooperate with you could seriously jeopardise the agreement.

It's not easy to negotiate with someone who is tough to work with. It could be upsetting and lead to needless arguments. It's critical to be able to control your emotions in these circumstances in addition to having techniques to assist you deal well with challenging individuals. It might be difficult to maintain self-control in any high-stress circumstance.

Because it sometimes feels very personal, negotiating with a difficult person can be very challenging. However, it's usually not personal. This means that you may control your tension and prevent feeling overwhelmed by managing and regulating your own emotions during these conversations.

Applying Sunnah-based Strategies to Navigate Tough Negotiations

The Sunnah holds great significance in Islam as a source of wisdom, understanding, and inspiration for Muslims worldwide. The teachings, deeds, and sayings of the Prophet Muhammad (PBUH) form the basis of the Sunnah, which provides Muslims with invaluable guidance on upholding Islamic values and leading moral lives.

Although navigating difficult negotiations can be difficult, using Sunnah-based tactics can offer an ethical and disciplined framework for reaching a polite and successful conclusion. The following Sunnah-based tactics will help you get through challenging negotiations:

Purifying the intention

The Prophet Muhammad (PBUH) constantly sought Allah's blessings by basing both his words and deeds on noble intentions. He always saw the positive side of every outcome that resulted from his sermons. In his hadith, the Prophet Muhammad (PBUH) made the following statement about the significance of intention:

> "Indeed, every deed is based on intention, and people will act according to their intentions." (Sahih Al-Bukhari)

Make sure that your objective is to establish an arrangement that benefits everyone in addition to achieving personal advantage before you enter the discussion.

Think before you speak.

Gaining control over our emotions is the first step towards crafting the best speech. Not that we are emotionless, but rather that we don't become enraged when we are aroused. The Prophet (PBUH) will constantly counteract evil with good. If we encounter any difficulties throughout the negotiation, we must act similarly.

If you don't communicate calmly and clearly during a negotiation, the other person might not understand what you're saying, which could irritate you later on if they don't follow your instructions. It needlessly causes friction. As a result, speak in a clear, succinct, and understandable manner.

Hazrat Aishah (RA) said:

> "The Messenger of Allah (PBUH) did not speak quickly like you do now rather, he would speak so clearly,

unmistakably, and that those who sat with him would memorise it." (Tirmidhi)

Think About Mutual Gain

The goal of negotiations should be to bring about advantages for each and every party. Seeking solutions that benefit everyone is something that the Prophet (PBUH) strongly advocated.

Pay Close Attention

Use the proportions of your four senses—two ears, two eyes, and one mouth—while negotiating. This is known as the 80/20 rule: 20 per cent talking and 80 per cent listening. Your client will provide you with useful signals and information as they are speaking, including their financial line. All you can do while you're speaking is confirm what they already know or divulge fresh information that you would prefer they don't know and that might be harmful to you.

Active listening

The purpose of listening to the Prophet (PBUH) was to comprehend what the other person was saying. He wasn't listening; he wasn't preoccupied with formulating a mental response. He was interested in learning the other person's perspective.

This is demonstrated in his dialogues with those around him, and it serves as a reminder to pay attention to what people are saying and refrain from judging them before they have spoken. After hearing their entire speech, the Prophet (PBUH) would ask if they had anything else to say. That is when he would respond.

Practicing Patience

In Islam, patience is highly valued and is crucial during discussions. It promotes understanding and, by making room for discussion and compromise, can result in better outcomes. Perhaps the most important quality of a skilled negotiator is patience.

Time is equal to patience, and longer negotiations may result in greater results. Since patience grants you the advantage of time, it's the super negotiation tactic. It takes time to comprehend the specifics of the offer and the associated dangers.

Sincerity and Openness

In Islam, being genuine and honest is highly valued. Building trust and respect during negotiations by being open and honest about goals, capacities, and constraints paves the way for fruitful commercial partnerships.

By incorporating these Sunnah-based tactics, you can handle difficult negotiations with integrity and respect and have a better chance of reaching an agreement.

Chapter 7
Ethics of Contractual Agreements

Elements of an Islamic Contract

Shariah's word for contract, "aqd", means a tie or knot that holds two people together. Unlike English law, which was created by judges, the Islamic law of contracts was created by Fuqaha (jurists), following the rules set out in the Quran and stories told by the Prophet (PBUH). A contract, in this context, is a written statement of an offer and an acceptance.

Shariah specifies what can and can't happen for a deal to be valid. According to Shariah, any agreement meeting the necessary requirements is considered valid and legal. Over the course of Islamic culture, Islamic financial contracts have evolved to meet the changing needs of society.

If you read classic fiqh law books, "aqd" also refers to a contract, signifying "to tie" or "to end." Formally, it can be thought of as an offer and acceptance that binds both parties legally.

Shariah law says that there are a few things that must be true for a contract to be legal, such as the offeror, the acceptor, the subject of the offer, and the amount of money being paid. For a contract to be valid, two or more people must legally be able to sign it.

According to Islamic law, a person can only do business with others if they are mature and wise. Under Shariah law, the first part of a legal relationship is the offeror and the offeree. The individuals who sign a contract must be legally competent to agree to its terms.

> *"Observe the orphans through testing their abilities until they reach the age of marriage; then if you find them capable of sound judgment, hand over to them their property." (Quran 4:6)*

This indicates that caution and puberty are principal factors dictating one's competence to engage in transactions under Islamic law.

The capacity to possess is the most important factor for each party involved. Shariah 'Islamiyyah, has been characterised as having tremendous potential (ahliyyah). Consequently, Islamic scholars define capability as a characteristic that enables a person to earn rights and fulfil duties.

The second component of a permissible encounter under Islamic law is offering (referred to as *'ijab*) and accepting (referred to as *qabul*). An offer is a specific action that, based on the language of one of the contractual parties, presumes the permission or willingness of the person who initiated the action. Offers may be made orally or in writing; both forms are acceptable.

The word "qabul," which literally translates to "acceptance," refers to a statement made to indicate approval of the *'ijab* (offer). Muslim jurists generally interpret *qabul* in one of two basic ways.

Regardless of the sequence of events, most people believe that *qabul* is established by either the person who is the buyer or the person to whom the contract is intended. The Hanafi School, on the other hand, adopts a more moderate approach when it comes to defining *qabul* as a word that is uttered later and relates to future conditions.

Additionally, either the buyer or the seller can deliver *qabul*. This aspect incorporates elements of common law. Offers and acceptances may also take place via representatives or by modern communication means such as telex, fax, phone, and email.

Following the principles of Shariah law, the third component of a contract is the subject matter, also known as *mahal al-'aqd*. This refers to money or goods which must be lawful. The term "mal" refers to a resource that may be set aside for use when required. Commonly translated as "property," "mal" refers primarily to tangible things that can be observed in the outside world. In other words, it includes things that are sold, fixed and individually traceable as indicated at the sale.

A place or point of reference (*mahal al-'aqd*) relevant to the subject matter of the contract is required to be included in the document. The subject matter of a contract serves as its point of reference because this is where the rules of the contract are applied, ensuring they don't contradict the aims of the contract. The Islamic legal system places a significant amount of importance on the validity, existence, deliverability, and exactness of the subject matter.

Lawfulness requires that the object of exchange be lawful. This means both the subject matter of the object and the underlying reason must have legal value. The parties involved must be the rightful proprietors of the *qabd* object for a contract to be valid. The existence of concerns must be present at the time of the contract. Additionally, to be able to be delivered with absolute certainty, the object must also have its primary characteristics, quantity, and value properly determined.

According to Islamic law, the subject matter of a contract may contain advantages such as rent and physical property such as sales or mortgages.

Both the transaction and the contract are void if the subject's nature does not permit this form of transaction. For example, a contract involving the sale of endowed property is void, but a contract concerning its rental is legitimate and appropriate. Subject matter must meet many requirements to be considered valid:

- It must be relevant.

- It must be determinable.

- It must be able to be delivered.

- It must exist.

Islamic law allows pricing to be considered as another commodity rather than only a monetary value. In accordance with the Islamic ban on uncertainty, the price must be known and agreed upon at the time of the contract. It can't be fixed later using the market price, nor can it be left to the judgment of a third party.

In the context of Shariah law, legal ability (*ahliyyah*) is the fourth component of a valid contract. One of a contract's components, capacity, grants legal rights, promotes reciprocal advantages, and makes it easier for the parties to impose responsibilities on one another. Only with the capacity to contract can there be the right to contract and responsibilities.

According to Shariah law, for someone to lawfully complete a legal transaction, they must first reach the equivalent of majority in terms of both physical and intellectual maturity. This means that to fully realise their potential, a person must reach puberty and exercise sound judgment, also known as prudence.

General Islamic Rules Concerning Contracts

According to Imam Ghazali, "A Muslim who resolves to pursue trade as a profession or establish their own business should initially attain a comprehensive comprehension of the regulations governing business transactions as outlined in Islamic Shariah. Without such comprehension, they risk straying from the right path and committing serious transgressions, thus rendering their earnings unlawful."

Everyone should be aware of a few general guidelines about trade agreements. In these agreements, we are all participants, either directly or indirectly. As mentioned, clarity is one of the main problems.

Many hadiths about purchasing and selling suggest that the agreement must be very clear:

> Ibn 'Umar (R.A) narrated that the Prophet Muhammad (PBUH) said, "If palm trees are sold after they have been pollinated, the fruit belongs to the seller unless the buyer makes a stipulation about the inclusion."
> (Sahih Muslim)

> Hakim bin Hizam (R.A) narrated that the Prophet Muhammad (PBUH) said, "Both parties in a busi-

ness transaction have the right to annul it so long as they have not separated; and if they speak the truth and make everything clear, they will be blessed in their transaction; but if they tell a lie and conceal anything, the blessing on their transaction will be blotted out." (Sahih Muslim)

Ibn 'Umar (R.A) also related that the Prophet Muhammad (PBUH) forbade the sale of fruits until they were clearly in good condition, prohibiting it both for the seller and the buyer. (Sahih Muslim)

Jabir bin 'Abdullah (R.A) related that the Prophet Muhammad (PBUH) forbade the sale of a heap of dates, the weight of which is unknown, based on the known weight of dates. (Sahih Muslim)

Islamic traders ought to embrace many distinctive behaviours, unlike the ones adopted in the West. Furthermore, these manners are directly derived from the teachings of Prophet Muhammad (PBUH), not just a code of ethics for gentlemen. Buying and selling with any unfair advantage over other traders is prohibited. Trading without knowledge of current market pricing is one example.

Abu Hurayrah (R.A) related that the Prophet Muhammad (PBUH) said, "Do not meet the merchant on the way and enter into a business transaction with him, and whoever meets him and buys from him (and in case it is done, see) that when the owner of the merchandise comes into the market (and finds that he has been paid a lower price) he has the option (to declare the transaction null and void)." (Sahih Muslim)

Abu Hurayrah (R.A) related that the Prophet Muhammad (PBUH) said, "The townsman should not sell to a man from the desert (with a view to taking advantage of his ignorance of the market conditions of the city)." (Sahih Muslim)

Ibn 'Umar (R.A) related that the Prophet Muhammad (PBUH) said, "No one amongst you should enter into a transaction when another is bargaining." (Sahih Al-Bukhari)

Ibn 'Umar (R.A) related that the Prophet Muhammad (PBUH) said, "A person should not enter into a transaction when his brother is already making a transaction and should not make a proposal of marriage when his brother has already made a proposal except when he gives permission." (Sahih Al-Bukhari)

These two final hadiths have many consequences for sales, including the possibility of Muslim involvement in auctions and gazumping—raising the price of something after settling on a lower price.

Purchasing and selling involve a contract. These activities shouldn't be viewed as boring and routine processes. Instead, they are acts of worship—common human behaviours—that can bring numerous benefits in this life as well as the next. Moreover, the opposite is true. One is sinful if one carries out the act of purchasing or selling in a way that is against the law.

Nowadays, Islam is not taken into account when signing contracts, which is entirely inappropriate. The teachings found in the Quran and Sunnah are still relevant today, even though they did not entail camels, dates, or slaves when Prophet Muhammad (PBUH) lived. As Muslims, we shouldn't take any agreement lightly or assume that just because something is done in a certain manner now, it must be done that way, too.

Lastly, we should remind ourselves of the one obligatory contract that none of us are performing today: the contract of bayah to the Khaleefah.

> Ibn 'Umar (R.A) related that the Prophet Muhammad (PBUH) said, "Whosoever takes off his hand from allegiance (bayah), Allah will meet him on the Day of Resurrection without having any proof for himself, and whosoever dies while there was no allegiance on his neck dies a death of the Days of Ignorance (jahiliyyah)."
> (Sahih Muslim)

Prohibited Elements in Contractual Negotiations

The prohibition of Maysir and Gharar

This Arabic word *gharar* means "deceit, risk, fraud, uncertainty, or hazard that might result in destruction or loss." It's a very broad term. In Islamic law, *"gharar"* is any deal between possible things whose presence or description isn't clear because the parties lack sufficient information about the nature and quality of the item being contracted for or the final outcome. The Prophet (*PBUH*) prohibited practices such as buying young animals while they were still in their mothers' wombs, selling milk from cows without measuring it, buying war booty before distribution, acquiring charity gifts before receipt, and buying a diver's catch.

Islam strictly forbids business deals that hurt or exploit any party to a contract. The goal is to ensure honesty and safety by disallowing *gharar* in any business deals that involve risk, uncertainty, or guesswork about the important parts of the deal for either side or when there's doubt about a party's ability to fulfil their promises. All Islamic business and financial deals must be based on honesty, openness, and sharing of all important information. This is to make sure that no one has an unfair edge over anyone else.

Gharar is prohibited from ensuring that both sides of a deal are completely happy and in agreement. Full transparency and clarity are required, and both parties must fully understand the values being exchanged. The limit established by *gharar* protects against unplanned losses and possible disagreements about whether information is correct or missing.

Instead, Shariah law instructs banks and business owners to share gains and losses to build community and support collaborative business practices. Mutual risk-sharing can help spread the burden of loss by making sure that everyone is fairly exposed to risk. Risk and doubt, on the other hand, rely on how right and sufficient the facts are for making reasonable guesses about what will happen. Uncertainty or risk that is accepted can't be part of a contract.

Islam also strictly forbids gambling in all its manifestations. In Islam, gambling transactions such as *maysir* and *qimar* are deemed completely unfair. Maysir refers to the effortless accumulation of money through luck, whether or not it violates another person's rights. Qimar is the term for the game of chance, where winners benefit at the expense of losers.

While gambling is essentially speculative, commercial activities of any kind have no place in Islam because gambling is simply speculative. What Shariah forbids is speculation akin to gambling, where profit is pursued without honest effort or fair dealings. In this context, the buyer is not stealing someone else's property dishonestly; rather, they are dealing with the intention of generating a profit.

Prohibition of Riba

In Islam, all kinds of unearned income are forbidden, including interest, which is called "*riba*." Even though the Quran doesn't name a specific type of *riba*, Muslim scholars have made a distinction between the two: *Riba al-nasiah* and *Riba al-fadl*.

Riba al-nasiah refers to loan interest. In Islam, it's generally illegal to promise a good return on a loan ahead of time as a prize for waiting.

Riba al-fadl is the surplus paid on top of a loan. It means the bankrupt pays the borrower more money in exchange for similar things.

Shariah wants to get rid of all kinds of unfair business deals, not just the kind of mistreatment that is built into the system of interest.

Muslims believe that charging interest goes against the spirit of sharing and working together in business and that lending money on interest is not really business in the truest sense of the word. This is true even though interest is a big part of today's economy and is what keeps financial institutions going.

Islam knows that the kind of profit that comes from trade is fundamentally different from the kind of profit that comes from interest charges. That's why it allows trade but forbids interest. Interest-based deals might not allow for a fair profit split between the buyer and the seller. In trade, sellers profit from their efforts in acquiring goods, and buyers profit from subsequently selling those goods.

In addition, interest-based deals can perpetuate debt indefinitely since interest accrues as long as the loans remain unpaid. In the worst cases, this could lead to decades of debt that can't be paid back.

According to the Islamic economic system, interest shouldn't be allowed because risk-reward sharing is a better way to make things fair and urge people to be businesses. Conversely, interest-based banking systems put too much weight on collateral and fail to adequately consider the feasibility and how the project is or how the money will be used.

While cash flow and security are needed to ensure that the loan is paid back, placing too much weight on these factors obscures the true purpose of borrowing. This approach tends to perpetuate uneven capital distribution by disproportionately benefiting the rich, who typically have greater access to security and cash flow.

Therefore, Islam considers interest-based loans for business investments unfair because possible profits are uncertain and can't be guaranteed in advance. Also, if the business fails despite the entrepreneur's efforts and risks, they are obligated to pay the full amount of the loss. In contrast, the moneylender, who assumes less risk and effort, can easily benefit from a positive rate. According to Islam, everyone should share the gains and risks.

Also, middle-class customers and developing countries risk getting stuck in a never-ending circle of debt because creditors can make money off of interest without caring about the debtor's ability to pay it back. The Riba system also limits the resources that can be used for growth and puts the focus on macroeconomics, inflation, and foreign deficits because it encourages people and states to spend more than they earn. This makes some less developed countries use too many of the Earth's resources, which hurts the ecosystem.

In addition, the high interest rate fluctuations in modern economies make the investment markets unpredictable. This makes it hard for business owners to make choices and have a long-term investment plan. The rise in fake assets and the uncertainty of the financial markets often make economic upheaval worse.

Chapter 8
Negotiating Halal Business Transactions

Upholding Halal Transactions

In Islam, honesty in business is emphasised more than in any other faith because Islam controls and directs everything in life. It's not merely a personal belief system that has nothing to do with his political and economic life, like a modern man's faith.

It's not just a bunch of ideas or traditions and rites; it's a real rule that controls every part of life. It rules control our daily lives, politics, and relationships with other people just as much as they control business.

Islam principles vehemently condemn social injustices, dishonesty, political trickery, and economic mistreatment. In fact, fairness, honesty, and brotherhood are the building blocks of a real Islamic society. Any kind of dishonesty is entirely unacceptable. This is why the Holy Prophet (PBUH) emphasised being completely honest in business and trade.

It would not be too much of an exaggeration to say that total honesty is an important part of Islamic business and trade. The Prophet (PBUH) encouraged his followers to engage in trade ethically, viewing it not only as an occupation but as a means to uphold moral values and contribute positively to society.

In Islam, food that is legally obtained is very valuable. Faithful people believe that just as consuming unhealthy food can harm physical health, acquiring food unlawfully or dishonestly can damage moral and spiritual well-being. If a man lives off of the money he got dishonestly or illegally, he can't grow morally or spiritually.

Understanding the term *Haram*, which means "illegal" in an Islamic context, provides a better idea of the high moral standards Muslims are expected to uphold. If businesses carefully adhere to Islamic business principles, there would be no room for any kind of dishonesty in the marketplace, from the most obvious and direct business fraud to the subtle, deceptive practices often perceived as legitimate.

Islam vehemently condemns commercial dishonesty and illicit gains, categorically prohibiting all transactions that are not founded on justice and fair play. While chastising the dishonest dealer, the Holy Prophet (PBUH) uttered the words,

> *"Whosoever deceives us is not one of us."(Sahih Muslim)*

In his writings, Imam Ghazali says that any Muslim who wants to work in trade or start his own business must first learn all of the rules that guide business deals in Islamic Shariah. If he doesn't know this, he will make big mistakes that will make his gains illegal. In history, no one has ever put as much value on legal trade as the early Muslims did, and no other country has ever been so against illegal trade as they were. Because of this, al-Ghazali said that people who want to go into trade or business as a job should really learn about the rules and laws that govern these activities.

Importance of Fairness in Business Dealings

The Holy Quran emphasises the crucial importance of justice in business:

> *"O my people, gives full measure and weight justly and defrauds not men of their things, and act not corruptly in the land making mischief. What remains with Allah is better for you if you are believers."(Quran 11:85)*

These are Hazrat Shuaib's (R.A) comments to his people, summarising the essential business ideas in the Holy Quran.
1. Provide precise weight and measure.
2. Do not deprive someone of what is rightfully theirs.
3. Refrain from causing harm to the planet to cause trouble.
4. Be happy with the leftover money God gives us after giving others their fair share.

This text tells us that trade can grow when there's safety and peace. As a result, it urges people not to upset the peace of the land so that trade between different parts of the world can continue freely. We must be completely open and honest in business deals, giving others everything they deserve.

The Quran teaches us that the only legal profit God will bless is the one earned through honest dealings. We shouldn't be greedy or try to make money for ourselves. The rules against corruption and unfair practices in the Holy Book make it impossible to do anything illegal or unfair. It's important to remember that being fair is a noble quality, and giving others fair measure and weight means we must be fair and just in all our relationships.

Shuaib (R.A) stressed that both the buyer and the seller should understand and care for each other. It's wrong for one person to take unfair advantage of another person's lack of knowledge or simplicity. Sellers shouldn't overcharge buyers but must be fair and responsible and give the buyer what is rightfully theirs.

Islam tells its followers to treat others with kindness and fairness, vehemently opposing all kinds of exploitation and unfair advantage-taking. No deal can be made without this fair idea. Often, illegal deals are made out of a desire for money or a bad desire to move up in society.

Islam gives us a different way to judge someone's rank that goes after the source of our desire for money. The Holy Quran says that morals and faith are the ways to tell if someone is good or bad. It admonishes against excessive wealth accumulation and greed.

In Islam, the most religious individuals are viewed as the most noble in the sight of God. In every way, Islam makes it harder to give in to the urge to do illegal business and crime. Now, let's discuss the types of business activities that are prohibited in Islam. The Holy Prophet (PBUH) established some rules that all transactions must follow.

The Fundamental Requirements in Islamic Business Transactions

Items are bought and sold, with money formally transferred to ownership. Clarity is crucial regarding the goods being sold and the corresponding payment. According to this principle, the goods sold must have been properly obtained.

Selling stolen or dishonestly obtained goods is not permissible in lawful business practices. Similarly, using unlawfully obtained money or proceeds from illegal activities as payment is prohibited. Both buyers and sellers are responsible for ensuring the legality of both the goods and the funds involved. Transactions should take place in open markets where goods and products are openly offered for sale. Before buyers make offers, the seller or their representatives should know how the market is doing. This knowledge is essential for sellers to protect themselves from being exploited.

Selling things before full acquisition is discouraged in Islam. The Holy Prophet (PBUH) cautioned Muslims against engaging in advance negotiations, which may be defined as the act of purchasing goods before one has complete control over one's possessions. In accordance with the teachings of the Holy Prophet (PBUH),

> *"Whoever buys cereals shall not tell them until he has obtained their possession." (Sahih Muslim)*

Ibn Abbas has asserted that the laws applicable to wheat are also applicable to other fields of endeavour. It was already said by the Holy Prophet (PBUH) that one shouldn't bargain over anything that is not with them. This indicates that you shouldn't engage in any transactions or exchanges prohibited by Islamic law.

Trading is restricted to just those commodities and items certified halal, which literally translates to "lawful." To engage in commerce or to sell items that violate the precepts of Islam is a violation of the faith.

For example, it's against the law to trade gods, pigs, wine, and animal corpses.

A reputable Muslim businessman would not even trade in such goods since it's against the law for ladies to wear garments that are too thin or see-through. This is because it's considered a violation of the law. It's not possible to sell the body of an animal. However, he is unable to flay the flesh of the deceased animal. The skin, which can be sold since it may be used to create shoes, is unavailable for flaying. The tusks of an elephant are similar to the skin of other animals in that they may be used in many ways.

Prohibited Forms of Business

Speculative trading is motivated by self-interest, involving the practice of purchasing large quantities of goods at a low cost and selling them later at high prices, often manipulating the entire market for personal gain. This behaviour demonstrates that speculators prioritise their own financial gain over the broader welfare of society. Speculators aim to artificially incite a shortage of goods and commodities to put the economy under inflationary pressure, which ultimately affects the impoverished masses. Islam denounces such speculative trade.

Islam allows trading as long as it follows the Sunnah and the Quran's rules. In fact, Islam has made it illegal to lie or be dishonest in business deals. It doesn't allow transactions that even slightly resemble scams. Traders have been taught that useless or broken items should never be traded for useful or fixed ones, and buyers should be aware of any problems with the goods they buy.

The Prophet (PBUH) said: "The buyer and the seller have the option of cancelling the contract as long as they have not separated; then. If they both speak the truth and make manifest, their transaction shall be blessed, and if they conceal and tell lies, the blessing of their transaction shall be obliterated."

Monopoly business: Monopolies result in the concentration of supply in the hands of a single party and exploit consumers and workers. The Holy Prophet (PBUH) declared them to be illegal. In Islamic civilisation, monopolies, cartels, and enormous trusts shouldn't exist. The economic system controlled by monopolies undermines the goal of maximum social advantage that Islamic society aspires to, as it demonstrates a lack of harmony between private and public interests.

Transactions with a gambling-like quality: Maisir, which literally translates to "getting something too easily" or "getting a profit without working for it," is the Arabic word for gambling. The term's precise interpretation clarifies the rationale behind Islam's ban on gambling. Any financial benefit that is too easy to obtain—that is, one doesn't have to labour for it—is illegal.

As long as the Holy Prophet (PBUH) was living, Arabs' favourite way to gamble was to draw lots with arrows from a bag. People who drew some blank ones didn't get anything. Some talked about gifts, no matter how big or small they were.

Unless someone was lying, the only thing that determined whether someone got something or nothing was luck. The movement against gaming is based on the idea that you can win something you haven't earned or lose something by pure luck. Gambling includes dice, raffles, prize bonds, and bets on horse races.

Exchanges based on interest: In Islam, any deal that involves interest is illegal. Some people have a hard time following the rule that says you can't charge interest because they think interest and trade profit are the same. When you put money into a bank account, you get interest, but when you put money into trade, you get something extra called profit.

For what reason should one kind of excess be okay while the other is not? They don't see the main difference between the two. When you trade, you could lose money. In this case, the entrepreneur's innovation, hard work, and speed all add to the profit, not just the amount of money they put in. Because of this, its rate can't be set in stone. Commerce also brings about effects.

Someone who has worked hard and been through pain gets something. It helps the economy grow and creates jobs for everyone. It will also be shown that trade is a big part of a progressing society because it helps people and shares ideas. Islam and Islamic culture are spreading around the world. Muslim merchants have been significant in the Far East. Interest doesn't have many good points.

The steady rate of return an owner gets from a business venture without taking any risk of losing money and without having to work hard to increase it encourages people to be cheap, selfish, and heartless, like Shylock. When it comes to the economy, it both starts and makes problems worse. As a result, Islam has correctly banned all deals based on or involving it in any way.

These are all examples of illegal business deals: borrowing money with interest, keeping deposits in a bank to earn interest, getting discounts on goods or commodities in exchange for upfront price payments, mortgaging and using property that makes money against a set amount that must be paid back in full when the property is redeemed, and investing money in a trade against a set rate of profit.

Munabadha and Mulamasa: In addition to establishing rules for trade and bartering, Islam also banned two types of sales contracts that were used before its advent. In both situations, the buyer did not have a chance to check out the item before purchase. Munabadha refers to a practice in which the customer acquires the fabric without the opportunity to look it over carefully. Mulamasa means "just touching the cloth to seal the deal," which is the act of touching a piece of clothing without looking at it very closely.

These types of deals were prohibited because they prevented the customer from seeing the goods first, leading to the possibility of one party unfairly losing out on the deal.

Islam actually advocates buying goods and commodities in the open market, ensuring fairness and transparency. When making offers to buy towns or goods in bulk, the seller or his agents must be told how the market is doing. He shouldn't be caught off guard in case someone takes advantage of his ignorance. All of this is very clearly stated by the Prophet (PBUH).

As mentioned earlier, Islam seeks to be fair to everyone involved in a deal. It's wrong for one person to do something that helps him but hurts the other person. It's not fair for the buyer to take advantage of the seller's lack of knowledge; instead, sellers should inform buyers about any problems with the goods. This mutual transparency ensures that all transactions are just and fair.

Muzabana: In Mozambique, people trade fresh fruit for dry fruit. The amount of dry fruit is weighed and set, but the amount of fresh fruit that is to be traded is guessed while still on the trees. The Holy Prophet (PBUH) prohibited this deal because it was like jumping into the dark, as no one knew how much fruit was actually on the trees.

Mu'awamas: This entails selling the fruit while it's still on the trees for a duration of one, two, or three years, even before it's visible. It's forbidden because, similar to Muzabana, it's a leap into the unknown and can lead to resentment and frustration.

Bai' al-Gharar: This is the sale of something one neither owns nor expects to control, such as fish in a river or birds in the sky. Having possession is one of the prerequisites for a sale. Anything that is not in one's possession can't be sold.

Bai' al-'Uryan: This involves purchasing something in exchange for a small advance under the condition that the advance will be adjusted if a deal is signed, and the seller will promptly return the advance if the deal is cancelled. Since the advance is small, the buyer's liability is almost nonexistent. If the agreement benefits him, he will follow through on it; if not, he will back out of it.

Bai' al-Mudtar: This is the act of purchasing something under duress or when the owner feels pressure to sell. Instead of taking advantage of the seller's distress, one should assist the seller rather than buy the item and unfairly profit from his inability.

Bai' alal-Bai': This refers to selling above and beyond another sale. When one party sells goods to another, a third party shouldn't break the agreement by attempting to sell their goods at a reduced price or by pointing out flaws in the items. The Prophet (PBUH) stated, "A Muslim shouldn't purchase in opposition to his brother, nor should he send a marriage proposal over and above the proposal of another."

Bai' al-Hast: Also known as pebble-based sales, the buyer or seller indicates agreement by tossing a pebble onto the merchandise, or the seller informs the buyer that whatever is hit by the stone will be sold to them. A sale contract is a serious subject, and it shouldn't be completed with haphazard techniques like slinging pebbles upon the merchandise. It's forbidden to finalise a deal in this manner since it could cause unfairness and hardship to one party.

Unripe maize and fruit sales: Hazrat Anas (RA) states that the Holy Prophet (PBUH) forbade selling maize before it ripened, grapes before they turned dark and uncooked dates. Date palm fruit shouldn't be sold until it turns red or yellow.

This is a quick summary of the sales transactions that Islam forbids. After considering the types of transactions mentioned above and going into further depth in "Kitab al-Buyu," the following conclusions can be drawn:

1. In business interactions, Islam demands complete justice and fairness.

2. An individual hasn't struck a decent deal in the eyes of Islam if they compromise their faith and forfeit their Lord's favour to obtain financial advantage. A Muslim would never accept such a lousy deal. A Muslim businessman doesn't worship money nor have an excessive passion for wealth. Above all, he values morality, piety, and faith.

3. The Islamic faith doesn't believe that all business dealings are fair and that all forms of cunning and dishonesty are acceptable. Islam views trade and business as an economic activity that should be conducted with humanity in mind, emphasising justice and fairness. It doesn't support ruthless rivalry, as this idea is fundamentally anti-Islamic.

4. According to Islamic law, both the buyer and the seller should regard one another as fellow Muslims or people, making every effort to support and assist one another. In the event that the seller overcharges the consumer, he ought to make up for the excessive amount paid rather than taking pride in his cunning move.

5. All agreements that are tightened without allowing the buyer an opportunity to inspect the items thoroughly are forbidden since doing so would deprive him of a right that was rightfully his.

6. Forceful transactions and those in which the buyer unfairly benefits from the seller's incapacity or suffering are likewise discouraged.

7. The Islamic faith forbids the trade of wine, pigs, animal corpses, and other items whose usage is deemed Haram (illegal).

8. It has also outlawed the exchange of goods that degrade or corrupt Muslim culture.

Chapter 9
Advancing Negotiation Skills through Faith and Practice

Negotiation is both an art and a science, requiring a delicate balance between strategy, empathy, and ethics. For Muslim negotiators, integrating Islamic principles into negotiation practices offers a unique path to achieving success while upholding faith-based values. This chapter delves into the continuous journey of improving negotiation skills, inspired by Islamic teachings and the example of the Prophet Muhammad (PBUH).

Continual Improvement and Growth in Negotiation Skills

Committing to Lifelong Learning and Development Based on Islamic Principles

In Islam, the pursuit of knowledge is highly valued and encouraged. This principle extends to the development of negotiation skills. Committing to lifelong learning in this area involves:

Engaging in a quest for knowledge is foundational to honing negotiation skills. This pursuit involves immersing oneself in various educational avenues, such as books, seminars, and workshops.

> *"This commitment finds resonance in Islamic teachings, which advocate for continuous learning, echoing the Quranic injunction, 'Say, 'My Lord, increase me in knowledge'." (Quran 20:114)*

Moreover, the journey of growth entails reflecting on past negotiation encounters, drawing lessons from both triumphs and tribulations. Viewing these experiences through the prism of Islamic principles provides a profound understanding, enriching future negotiation endeavours.

Integral to this journey is the cultivation of patience and persistence, virtues extolled in Islam negotiation, often a test of endurance, benefits from these qualities, fostering outcomes that are effective and rooted in mutual respect.

Embracing Faith-Based Approaches to Negotiation for Personal and Professional Success

Faith-based approaches to negotiation integrate Islamic teachings and values, creating a framework that promotes personal and professional success. Key elements include:

Honesty and Transparency: Islam strongly emphasises honesty and transparency in all dealings. The Prophet Muhammad (PBUH) said,

> *"The truthful merchant is with the Prophets, the truthful, and the martyrs" (Tirmidhi)*

Being honest and transparent builds trust and fosters long-term relationships.

Fairness and Justice: Ensuring fairness and justice in negotiations aligns with the Quranic injunction,

> *"O you who have believed, be persistently standing firm in justice, witnesses for Allah, even if it be against yourselves or parents and relatives" (Quran 4:135)*

Striving for equitable outcomes benefits all parties involved.

Empathy and Compassion: Understanding and addressing the needs and concerns of others is a core Islamic value. The Prophet Muhammad (PBUH) exemplified this in his dealings, showing empathy and compassion even in challenging situations. This approach can lead to more amicable and successful negotiations.

Empowering Muslim Negotiators to Uphold Prophetic Values

Inspiring a New Generation of Ethical Negotiators Guided by Islamic Ethics

The next generation of Muslim negotiators can be empowered by drawing inspiration from the ethical teachings of Islam and the example of the Prophet Muhammad (PBUH). This involves:

Role Modelling: Experienced negotiators who exemplify Islamic ethics can serve as role models, demonstrating how to navigate complex negotiations with integrity and faith. Their behaviour can inspire and guide younger negotiators.

Mentorship and Guidance: Establishing mentorship programs where seasoned negotiators mentor emerging professionals can provide valuable support and guidance. These relationships can help instil strong ethical foundations and practical skills.

Community and Support Networks: Building strong community networks where Muslim negotiators can share experiences, challenges, and successes fosters a sense of solidarity and mutual growth. Such networks can provide moral and practical support.

Promoting the Transformative Impact of Sunnah-Based Negotiation Practices

The Sunnah, the exemplary practices of the Prophet Muhammad (PBUH), provides timeless guidance on conducting negotiations with integrity and wisdom. Embracing these practices aligns with Islamic principles and offers pragmatic benefits in achieving successful outcomes.

Firstly, highlighting success stories of negotiations guided by the Sunnah can serve as powerful testimonials to the effectiveness of faith-based approaches. By sharing narratives of individuals who have applied Prophetic teachings in their negotiations, others can be inspired and motivated to adopt similar practices.

These stories showcase how principles such as honesty, patience, and empathy, exemplified by the Prophet Muhammad (PBUH), can lead to mutually beneficial agreements and strengthened relationships. Moreover, these success stories illustrate the practical relevance of Sunnah-based negotiation techniques in diverse contexts, from business transactions to interpersonal disputes.

Secondly, educational initiatives are pivotal in equipping Muslim negotiators with the knowledge and skills to implement Sunnah-based approaches. Workshops, courses, and seminars focused on applying Prophetic principles in negotiation can provide participants with practical tools and strategies. These initiatives can be integrated into both professional development programs and religious education curricula, ensuring that individuals have access to comprehensive training in faith-based negotiation practices.

By incorporating experiential learning activities and case studies, participants can deepen their understanding of how Sunnah-based techniques can be effectively applied in real-world negotiation scenarios.

Furthermore, fostering research and publications on the intersection of Islamic principles and negotiation can contribute to this field's academic and practical understanding. Encouraging scholars to explore topics such as ethics in negotiation, conflict resolution in Islam, and the role of spirituality in decision-making can generate valuable insights and knowledge.

Academic journals, conferences, and research grants can provide platforms for scholars to disseminate their findings and engage in dialogues with practitioners and policymakers. Building a robust body of literature on faith-based negotiation practices can strengthen the legitimacy and relevance of these approaches, leading to broader acceptance and adoption within professional circles.

Advancing negotiation skills through faith and practice requires a commitment to continual learning and growth inspired by Islamic teachings. By embracing Sunnah-based approaches and upholding Prophetic values, Muslim negotiators can achieve personal and professional success while positively impacting their communities and beyond.

Through initiatives such as highlighting success stories, offering educational programs, and supporting research endeavours, the integration of Islamic principles into negotiation can be promoted, fostering greater harmony, justice, and integrity in the negotiation process. As individuals strive to emulate the noble character of the Prophet Muhammad (PBUH) in their interactions, they contribute to building a world characterised by compassion, fairness, and mutual respect.

Chapter 10
Conclusion

In this book we've embarked on a journey through Islam's rich teachings regarding negotiation, drawing upon the profound wisdom found in Prophetic traditions. Throughout this exploration, we've delved into various aspects of negotiation, from its fundamental principles to its practical application in business transactions and conflict resolution.

In the beginning, we discussed what communication means in Islam and how the lessons of the Prophet Muhammad (PBUH) can help us do it. Then, important rules of Islamic bargaining were explained, with a focus on the importance of being moral and building trust during talks.

Preparation and planning emerged as crucial components of successful negotiations, where we learned to apply Prophetic strategies to enhance our readiness for dialogue. Effective communication skills, both verbal and nonverbal, were highlighted as indispensable tools in achieving mutually beneficial outcomes.

In addressing conflicts, we explored the Prophetic approaches to resolution and the role of mediation in Islamic law. Additionally, we examined negotiation tactics and strategies, equipping us with the necessary tools to navigate challenging situations and negotiate with integrity.

Ethical considerations remained at the forefront of our discussions, particularly in contractual agreements, where we outlined the elements of an Islamic contract and cautioned against prohibited practices such as *gharar* and *maysir*. Furthermore, the importance of conducting halal business transactions with fairness and integrity was emphasised, focusing on upholding Prophetic values in all aspects of commerce.

Lastly, we concluded by reflecting on the continuous journey of growth and improvement in negotiation skills, recognising the pivotal role of faith and practice in empowering Muslim negotiators to embody the principles of Islam in their dealings.

In essence, this book serves as a comprehensive guide that synthesises timeless Islamic teachings with modern negotiation strategies to facilitate successful deals while upholding the ethical standards and values advocated by the Prophet Muhammad (PBUH) and to always keep faith at the forefront of all our dealings in our personal and professional lives.

Find Out More

Website: www.barakahinbusiness.com

Socials: @barakahinbusiness

If you enjoyed this book, kindly leave a review to help expand our reach so others may benefit also.

www.ingramcontent.com/pod-product-compliance
Lightning Source LLC
Chambersburg PA
CBHW070431010526
44118CB00014B/1994